GREAT ADVENTURES

GREAT ADVENTURES

SIGMUND BROUWER

Tyndale House Publishers, Wheaton, Illinois

Visit the exciting Web site for kids at www.cool2read.com

You can contact Sigmund Brouwer through his Web site at www.coolreading.com

Cover design by Luke Daab

Interior design by Beth Sparkman

Edited by Erin Keeley and Betty Free

Scripture quotations are taken from the *Holy Bible,* New Living Translation, copyright © 1996. Used by permission of Tyndale House Publishers, Inc., Wheaton, Illinois 60189. All rights reserved.

Library of Congress Cataloging-in-Publication Data

Brouwer, Sigmund, date.
   Great adventures : golden tonsils and other great stories / Sigmund Brouwer.
     p. cm.
Summary: Contains fifteen stories, each of which is the starting point for a five-day week's worth of devotions and discussion questions for the whole family.
   ISBN 0-8423-5239-2 (sc)
   1. Christian children—Prayer-books and devotions—English. [1. Prayer books and devotions.] I. Title
BV4870 .B683 2003
249—dc21   2002010959

ISBN 0-8423-5239-2

Printed in the United States of America

07   06   05   04   03
5   4   3   2   1

CONTENTS

Introduction vii
Are You Ready for a Lifetime of Adventure?

Week 1 1
Wild Ride *(Treating Others with Respect)*

Week 2 19
Dumb Brat *(Unselfishness)*

Week 3 37
Show-Off *(Pride)*

Week 4 57
A Small Wooden Cross *(Forgiveness)*

Week 5 79
A Hassrock Classic *(A Consistent Christian)*

Week 6 101
In the Garden *(A True Leader)*

Week 7 125
The Hardly Boys *(True Success)*

Week 8 145
Blow Out *(Respecting the Rules)*

Week 9 165
The Sweater *(God's Kind of Love)*

Week 10 185
Church Lady *(More on Love)*

Week 11 205
Things Unseen *(The Adventure of Faith)*

Week 12 225
Golden Tonsils *(How Honest Is Honest?)*

Week 13 245
Tommy's Shoes *(Being an Encourager)*

Week 14 267
Catacomb Glory *(Sold Out for Jesus)*

Week 15 287
Buffalo Soldier *(True Courage)*

ARE YOU READY FOR A LIFETIME OF ADVENTURE?

Jesus was a man of adventure—a true pioneer who fought and taught bravely. He was a man to follow and to become more like.

When Jesus spoke, people listened, whether they agreed with his teachings or not. How did he capture their attention? With stories called *parables*.

The fact that I have been to the shores of the Sea of Galilee helps me see the situation: Long, rolling hills edge the far horizon. Wind ripples the water, then the tall grass. There is the peace of nature's quiet. And near Capernaum where Jesus often taught, there is a place where the slope forms a perfect amphitheater.

Jesus would have stood at the base of the slope, with hundreds of people sitting in half circles that spread up the hill. His voice would have carried above the breeze to reach each of them clearly.

When I picture Jesus sharing his parables, my imagination is drawn to his audience. These were hungry people—not only physically, but spiritually. They traveled by foot for miles to hear him. Many were in poor health, their bodies weakened by years of hard work. Most didn't have much schooling. Hardly any could read.

How long would the people have sat if Jesus had spoken in words beyond their understanding? How long if he had not drawn them in so much that they forgot their aching muscles, tired bones, and grumbling stomachs? How long would they have remained if he had begun to lecture them until they began to squirm? How long if he had preached at them like their synagogue teachers did, burdening them with hundreds of rules?

Jesus knew the best way to reach his audience was through stories. The stories he told were powerful, often with unexpected twists. And, perhaps surprisingly, his stories rarely mentioned God or religion, yet they pointed out important truths. The lessons were "caught," not "taught," and they gave his listeners something to discuss with each other long after Jesus had left their area.

I understand the power of story. It is my prayer that the stories in this devotional will help readers today. The stories are set in situations that today's kids will find similar to their own circumstances. I hope parents will enjoy reading them aloud. Each story emphasizes a scriptural passage and is followed by thoughts and questions on the meaning of the story as it relates to that Scripture.

Each five-day week begins with an adventure story. Focusing on one theme from that story and three subtopics, the rest of the week is filled with in-depth questions, Scriptures, and prayers—even questions for kids to ask adults! Each week ends with creative application ideas.

Whether you are reading the 15 weeks of stories and daily devotional material as a family, as a small group, or on your own, I hope you will discover a sense of adventure that binds you to God. Knowing God and growing in faith are lifetime adventures. Enjoy the journey!

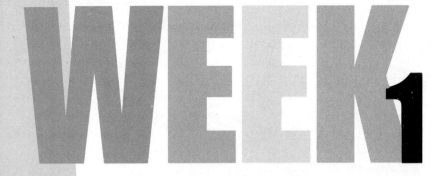

WHAT'S UP THIS WEEK:
Treating Others with Respect

THEME VERSES FOR THE WEEK:
Mark 12:29-31

Jesus replied, "The most important commandment is this: 'Hear, O Israel! The Lord our God
is the one and only Lord. And you must love the
Lord your God with all your heart, all your soul,
all your mind, and all your strength.' The second
is equally important: 'Love your neighbor as
yourself.' No other commandment is greater
than these."

Mike and Jimmy challenged the other kids to jump their bikes into the lake, but the two of them were the ones who ended up all wet. Find out what happens when a little less than total honesty, a couple of practical jokes gone wrong, and a bit too much bragging combine for a wild ride.

Wild Ride

Under a blue sky on the hottest day of the summer, only three of us remained at the top of the hill sitting on our mountain bikes.

On one side of me sat a girl who had just moved to town. A little way off, my best friend, Jimmy Evans, prepared to zoom down the steep slope.

Jimmy was far enough away that I could whisper to the girl, Suzy Wallace.

"You know what?" I said softly. "Last night I snuck into Jimmy's garage and loosened the pedals on his bike. He doesn't have a chance!"

"I thought he was your best friend," she whispered back.

"He is," I said. "Best friends since first grade."

Jimmy had no idea what we were

talking about. He grinned at me and yelled, "Ready, Mr. Loser?"

I looked down the bike path that headed straight toward the lake. A crowd of kids waited for the three of us to jump in the first annual Daredevil Mountain Bike Jumping Contest.

"Me? Mr. Loser?" I said to him. "The name's Mike Roberts, king of daredevils. You might remember that my practice jump yesterday cleared yours by half a mile."

Ever since we were little, Jimmy and I have competed against each other. Not in a bad way, like trying to hurt each other. But afterwards we like to brag. Anything we play—baseball, football, soccer—we always try to do better than the other guy.

Jimmy is tall and skinny, like me. People sometimes think we're brothers, because we both have the same reddish-blond hair . . . and maybe because we argue like brothers. Not in a bad way, though, because we really are friends.

"Ha ha. Half a mile if you measure backward," Jimmy shot back. "How 'bout the loser cuts the winner's lawn for the rest of the summer?"

I laughed. He, of course, didn't know why. Those pedals were going to come off as soon as he stepped down hard enough to get any speed.

"You got a deal," I said. "And Suzy's a witness. Right, Suzy?"

"Sure," she said. "But can I get in on this deal too?" Her question surprised us both.

"You guys aren't afraid of a girl beating you, are you?"

"No," I said quickly.

"No way," Jimmy added. "This whole contest was our idea."

4

▼ ▼ ▼ ▼ ▼

It was. We'd come up with the Daredevil Mountain Bike Jumping Contest because summers in Greenville are so boring.

I must admit, it was a good idea. A professional stunt rider
lives in our town, and he built a ramp next to the lake to
practice his bike tricks. The water's not deep enough that you
could lose a bike, and it isn't so shallow that a person could
get hurt jumping into it.

We asked his permission to use the ramp, then we told all
our friends. The idea was to ride down the hill as fast as possible, shoot off the ramp, and jump out over the lake as far
as you could.

Kids were allowed to practice all week; then on Saturday
we had started with 15 of us at the top of the hill.

The view was great. Our town reflected in the water on
the other side of the lake. Rolling hills spread off as far as you
could see. But nobody was looking at the scenery, because
we were all too nervous.

At the base of the hill, my sister and Jimmy's sister held
video cameras to tape the jumps, in case anybody disagreed
on who had jumped the highest and the farthest. Even our
parents came, just in case somebody got hurt.

We'd watched the first 12 jumpers go. Seeing kids hit the
ramp full speed on their mountain bikes and vault into the air
was great. Some held on to the handlebars as they hit the
water. Others jumped off their bikes for superbig splashdowns.

▼ ▼ ▼ ▼ ▼

"So what's your offer?" Jimmy asked Suzy.

"If I don't beat both of your jumps," she said, "I'll cut both
your lawns all summer."

"And if you somehow actually manage to beat us?" Jimmy asked.

"You visit me and my dad every Sunday morning for the rest of the summer."

"Huh?" Jimmy asked. "Your dad?"

"He's a minister. You guys will have to come to church."

"We don't need preaching," Jimmy said.

"Afraid?" She smiled and laughed.

"You're on," he said.

"You're on," I said.

Jimmy waved and pushed off.

I held my breath.

He's a great athlete. His legs are stronger than mine, and he's very coordinated. That's why he had a good chance of winning—except for those bike pedals.

A third of the way down, he pushed so hard that both pedals came off. He was standing as he pedaled, and he slammed down hard on the bike's crossbar. He barely kept his balance as he hit the ramp, but I could tell he was in pain by the way he fell over sideways in the air. Altogether, Jimmy cleared only five feet.

Before he got out of the water, I busted a gut laughing. Even from the top of the hill, I could hear his groans of pain.

"Mike Roberts, you dog!" he shouted. "I know it was you who did that!"

"Best friends, huh?" Suzy said.

"Sure," I grinned. "Such good friends that I'll beat you on this jump—and you can cut my lawn instead of him doing it."

She smiled. "Go for it."

"I will."

I got ready. From my practice runs, I knew how much fun this was going to be.

The key was to start fast and hard. There were no bumps to worry about on the way down. You could hit the ramp at full speed. As long as you dipped at the knees just before takeoff and kept your balance in the air, it was a breeze. Landing was fun too. The water really cooled you off.

"Well?" she said. "I'm waiting."

"Psyching myself up," I explained. "With Jimmy out of the way, I've got a real good shot at winning."

"Sure," she said with that smile.

I should have suspected something. But I was too dumb.

Standing, I slammed my feet down on the pedals as hard as I could. And halfway down, my bicycle chain snapped.

On the video Jimmy and I saw later, I looked exactly like he had. I fell hard on my bike seat, managed to keep my balance, hit the ramp and flew a few feet into the air. And, like Jimmy, I simply fell over sideways in a big whale splash.

I groaned as I came up for air. Only one person would have done this to me.

"Jimmy," I croaked. "I'll get you for this."

I dragged myself and my bike out of the water. But I was in too much pain to do much else as I flopped down beside Jimmy.

I groaned.

He groaned.

At the top of the hill, Suzy waved at both of us. She pushed off on her mountain bike, flashed down the hill, hit the ramp perfectly, and cleared enough air to easily win the contest.

"Remember," she said with that smile of hers. "See you Sunday morning."

"Yeah," Jimmy said.

"Yeah," I said.

As we watched her ride away, Jimmy groaned again. "You know," he said, "it was dumb of me to tell her ahead of time how I had fixed your chain to break halfway down the hill."

I shook my head. "Tell me about it."

We dragged ourselves home.

And Sunday morning?

Her father greeted us at the church and showed us to our seats.

You'd almost think Suzy had told him the whole story, because his sermon was about treating others with respect.

WHAT'S UP THIS WEEK?

Okay, so Mike and Jimmy didn't treat each other well. The big question now is, What did they do wrong? As this week continues, here's what we'll look at more closely:

- Honesty
- Bragging
- Taking Advantage of Others

PRAYER POWER

It's time to talk to God! Think about the story, and ask God to show you what he wants you to learn from it this week. The Holy Spirit will point out the truths he has for you, and he'll help you understand his ways.

HONESTY

You may have picked up on several ways that Mike and Jimmy weren't respectful of each other. Let's focus on honesty today.

BRAIN STRETCHERS
FOR KIDS:

1. What did you first think when you read about Mike's plan to trick Jimmy? Maybe you thought it was funny, or maybe you thought it was mean and saw a bad outcome from the beginning.
2. It's true: Practical jokes can be hilarious. But in what ways did Mike and Jimmy go too far in tricking each other?
3. How could the results of their trickery have been even more serious than they were?

ASK AN ADULT:

1. Was there ever a time when you took advantage of someone or felt taken advantage of? What were the results? a hurt relationship? guilty feelings?

SCRIPTURE POWER

Mike and Jimmy weren't respectful of each other; instead, they were dishonest. The Bible tells us how God feels about honesty and dishonesty:

> *The Lord hates cheating, but he delights in honesty. (Proverbs 11:1)*

"But I was just joking!" How many times have you heard someone say that? Yeah, we've all probably said it ourselves at one time or another. Of course, not all jokes are bad. But it's important to double check how someone else can be hurt. Both Mike and Jimmy could have wound up with more than just bruised limbs and egos.

Treachery and dishonesty are things that the Lord hates! The world has made these things an acceptable part of daily life, but those who love God are supposed to be different from the rest of the world! Change in our lives begins by first recognizing God's heart. By spending time with him, we can grow and become more like him.

> *Show respect for everyone. (1 Peter 2:17)*

Part of showing respect for everyone is respecting their trust in you. In other words, friends take a chance on trusting you to be honest. You don't want to mess with that! It can take a long time to earn back someone's trust after it's been broken.

PRAYER POWER

As you pray today, ask God to help you recognize the differences between being *almost* honest and being *truly* honest. It's often tough to recognize these differences! But if you ask him, God will develop the characteristic of honesty in you.

BRAGGING

Yesterday we discussed how honesty is part of treating others with respect. Today let's find out some things about controlling our words, particularly when it comes to bragging.

BRAIN STRETCHERS

FOR KIDS:

1. In "Wild Ride," can you tell what Suzy thought of Mike's and Jimmy's bragging about their plans to trick each other?
2. Why do you think that led her to help them change their focus?

ASK AN ADULT:

1. How can you tell the difference between a practical joke and trickery that goes too far?
2. Do you know anyone who brags a lot? Does that characteristic affect your opinion of him or her?

SCRIPTURE POWER

You call yourself a hero, do you? Why boast about this crime of yours, you who have disgraced God's people? All day long you plot destruction. Your tongue cuts like a sharp razor; you're an expert at telling lies. (Psalm 52:1-2)

Bragging is bad, and bragging about evil is even worse. In this passage the tongue is compared to a razor, a tool designed for cutting. We must make a choice about how we will use our tongue, whether to encourage people in a positive way or to hurt people in a cutting way.

We all make many mistakes, but those who control their tongues can also control themselves in every other way. (James 3:2)

Nobody's perfect. The tongue gets all of us into trouble. Controlling our lives, according to this verse, begins with controlling what we say. If we can get that under control, we will have the ability to control our actions, too. It's easy to end up in hot water because of our mouth. If we don't think before we speak, often the things that come out are not what we intend, and they hurt other people. It's been said that we've got one tongue and two ears for a good reason: so we'll listen twice as much as we talk!

The tongue is a small thing, but what enormous damage it can do. A tiny spark can set a great forest on fire. And the tongue is a flame of fire. It is full of wickedness that can ruin your whole life. It can turn the entire course of your life into a blazing flame of destruction, for it is set on fire by hell itself. (James 3:5-6)

The tongue is the strongest muscle in the whole body. It can destroy us if we don't control it! This paints a strong picture. Left unchecked, the tongue will cause a spark, which will create a forest fire of problems. But controlling our talk is so difficult that we can't do it on our own. Only God has the power to help us as we commit to him what we say every day.

PRAYER POWER

Praying for help to control our words is something most of us need to do often! Why not make a commitment to pray about it every day for two weeks or a month? You could tape a note to your mirror to remind yourself. Asking God on a daily basis to help you with your words will develop a great habit.

THURSDAY

TAKING ADVANTAGE OF OTHERS

All right, we've discussed honesty and bragging. What's next? How about not taking advantage of others? Let's think about how to define that. Taking advantage of someone means doing what you want to do without caring what the consequences might be for someone else. It also means looking out for yourself without considering others.

BRAIN STRETCHERS

FOR KIDS:

1. How did Mike and Jimmy try to take advantage of each other?
2. Have you ever felt taken advantage of by someone else? What happened?

ASK AN ADULT:

1. In what ways does God show us that he respects us? (Hint: Read John 3:16 and John 15:15.)
2. What are some ways we can give God our respect? (Hint: Think about the week's theme verse, shown on the next page.)

SCRIPTURE POWER

Let's review our theme verses for the week:

> Jesus replied, "The most important commandment is this:
> 'Hear, O Israel! The Lord our God is the one and only
> Lord. And you must love the Lord your God with all your
> heart, all your soul, all your mind, and all your strength.'
> The second is equally important: 'Love your neighbor as
> yourself.' No other commandment is greater than these."
> (Mark 12:29-31)

If we're following those directions from Jesus, we'll be careful
not to take advantage of other people. This is something
Mike and Jimmy must have forgotten about! They most definitely thought about themselves first. Besides those great
verses above, here's another one to think about:

> Since God chose you to be the holy people whom he
> loves, you must clothe yourselves with tenderhearted
> mercy, kindness, humility, gentleness, and patience.
> (Colossians 3:12)

Pretty clear, isn't it? Since God loves everyone equally, he
wants us to treat each other with all the kindness, humility,
gentleness, and patience that he shows to us every minute
of every day.

PRAYER POWER

The week is nearly over, and we've dug into some great
truths about honesty, controlling our tongue, and not taking
advantage of others. Today, ask God to reveal ways in which
you need to be more considerate of other people. You'll find
that it's one of the most important elements of showing
respect to them. Ask God for more sensitivity to recognize
others' needs and feelings.

FRIDAY

CONCLUDING THOUGHTS

Mike and Jimmy lost a bet with Suzy because they both told her a secret about the other. In addition to their loose lips, they both tried to cheat the other in an attempt to win the bike-jump contest. Suzy taught them both a lesson by using their secrets against them.

It's tempting to fall into the habits of dishonesty, bragging, and taking advantage of others. We cheat a little, lie a little, and tell ourselves it's all in fun. Nobody will get seriously hurt, and we were just joking, anyway! When we boil it down, however, we find that doing these things to people means that we value others less and ourselves more.

If you could tell Mike, Jimmy, or Suzy anything at all about what you've learned from their story, what would you say? What lesson hit home the most for you: honesty? controlling your tongue? not taking advantage of others?

LINE IT UP!

As you read the following situations, figure out why they are examples of less-than-respectful behavior toward others. Discuss what responses would have been better.

- You got invited to a party, but your best friend didn't. She asks you to do something that same night, but you tell her you're sick so her feelings won't be hurt because she wasn't invited.
- You make plans to play basketball with friends after school. As you run out the door, you notice your little sister crying on the front porch. You hurriedly ask her what's wrong. When she tells you about it, you give her a quick hug, tell her, "It's okay," and then book it down the street to meet your pals.
- Your mom has been really sick with the flu all week, but you planned a party with your friends this weekend. You feel bad for your mom, whose help you'll need. However, you really don't want to reschedule the party because the guy or girl you like has already said yes to coming, and you're not sure another weekend would work for him or her. So you keep the party plans.

PRAYER POWER

It's the end of the week, and hopefully you're feeling encouraged and challenged to apply some great lessons to your life. Why not take a moment to thank God for helping you grow? Then ask him to keep you sensitive to his leading as he teaches you to show respect for others through honesty, not bragging, and not trying to take advantage of people. His power can help you accomplish a lot!

WEEK 2

WHAT'S UP THIS WEEK:
Unselfishness

THEME VERSES FOR THE WEEK:
Philippians 2:3-6

Don't be selfish; don't live to make a good impression on others. Be humble, thinking of others as better than yourself. Don't think only about your own affairs, but be interested in others, too, and what they are doing. Your attitude should be the same that Christ Jesus had. Though he was God, he did not demand and cling to his rights as God.

A curious little brother and a model airplane combine for a crash landing when John loses his temper. Discover what he learns about taking time to care and putting others' needs first.

Dumb Brat

"John, when do fish sleep?"

"Huh?" I had my toothpick poised. Just a little dab of glue on the end, and I'd . . .

"I checked our goldfish. No eyelids. None of them."

"Yeah, yeah." I didn't dare wave Robbie away, not with a toothpick tipped with glue in one hand, not with the other holding the tiny pilot in the cockpit of the model airplane that I'd been working on every day after school over the last three weeks. *If either hand wavered even the slightest . . .*

"So if fish don't have eyelids, when do they sleep?"

"Aaargh!" I gritted my jaw and grunted in frustration, careful that the grunt did not shake my hands.

I eased the pilot into place. Released my hands. Held my breath. The pilot stayed.

Robbie tugged on my sleeve. I swiveled on my stool to face him.

He's eight years old—four years younger than I am. Wide, dark eyes. Shy smile. Skinny shoulders. Messy brown-black hair. Sloppy clothes. And a knack for bothering me.

Oh, I've tried to straighten him out.

I'll point to my closet. Shirts and pants hung neatly, *not* thrown into a heap on the floor like his are.

I'll point to his hair, a bird's nest. Not combed back, held in place with the gel I always offer to lend him.

I'll point to this den. Games on the shelf above the television. Videos stacked beside the VCR. Bookshelf behind me—books arranged in alphabetical order, with my model airplanes and model cars lined along the top, dusted once a week. I'll tell him this is the way the den should look *after* he's spent time in it, not before.

He'll just grin and nod.

Then I'll tell him it's real important, because now with Dad gone and Mom having to work full-time, it's up to us to maintain order in the house. I'll tell him that as good Christians, we should do our share without complaint.

And he'll just grin and nod. And be as messy as ever. And hound me whenever I'm at home, no matter how many times I've told him he's got to grow up and learn to do things on his own.

I repeated that lecture now, word by slow word—so he'd know how patient I was being despite his questions.

He just grinned and nodded. And stayed.

I dabbed my toothpick in the glue again. All I had left was the three-piece windshield. I'd already enameled the entire plane, afraid that if I painted after the windshield was in, I might get some on it. Once the windshield was in place, the

Spitfire—with a wingspan as wide as the table—would be finished. Hours and hours of delicate work, ready to be displayed on top of the bookshelf.

The phone rang as I picked up the first of the three pieces of clear plastic.

Robbie answered. It was my best friend, George, with math questions he couldn't understand on his homework. I set the toothpick down, happy to help. A guy doesn't get a reputation as the class brain without a little effort.

When I went back to my toothpick, the glue had dried in a clump on the end.

"Get me another, will ya?" Even without looking up, I knew Robbie was watching closely enough to know what I meant.

He handed me a clean toothpick.

"When *do* fish sleep?"

I sighed. "When they can't stay awake any longer."

"Oh."

I secured the left side of the windshield in place.

"John," Robbie blurted. "What about tennis balls?"

"For Pete's sake," I hissed. Did the centerpiece go in before the right-hand side? Or vice versa?

"Tennis balls. Why are they fuzzy? Why do dogs have black lips? Why are chalkboard erasers striped?"

Okay. Centerpiece first. Just a little more glue . . .

"And how do crickets make noise?"

I set the tiny piece of clear plastic down and faced him. "Robbie?"

He grinned that shy grin. "Yeah?"

For a second, I wanted to rub a hand affectionately over his messy hair, like Dad used to. But I could feel the glue on my fingers, and it put my mind back on the airplane.

I turned back, leaned over the cockpit and spoke without raising my head. "If I answer, will you leave me be?"

"Sure."

I began to move the centerpiece in place. "Crickets," I spoke in my most knowledgeable voice, "make noise by rubbing their legs together very rapidly."

Silence. Long enough for me to get the centerpiece fixed. *On to the very last piece of the hundreds of tiny pieces it had taken to make this work of art.*

"Do their legs get chapped?"

"What?!" I half shouted. If Mom were at home now, she'd have easily heard me from the kitchen.

"The crickets. Wouldn't all that rubbing give them chapped legs?"

I felt my hands shake with anger. How much patience should a guy have?

"Lubrication!" I shouted, desperate to silence him.

"Lubrication. Is that like oiling a door hinge?"

"Yes!" I roared. That was a mistake. My hand slipped, and the last piece smeared glue across the enamel.

Great. I'd probably have to repaint the entire front. If my hands had been around Robbie's throat, I'd have squeezed it into a toothpick to match the one now snapped in my fingers.

My hands only trembled slightly as I tried for the second time to put the last piece into place.

"Remember when Dad wanted a door to stop squeaking?" Robbie said. "He'd *oil* the hinges. So if a cricket has lubricated legs, then how can it make noise? I mean—"

I couldn't help myself. Why couldn't Robbie leave me alone, especially right when I needed to concentrate most? A sudden rage blurred my eyes and filled me so completely that even without knowing I was doing it, I was already turning and sweeping my right hand.

I caught a startled flash in his eyes before he ducked.

My hand slammed into the bookshelf behind him, crashed through a row of books with enough force to spray them onto the floor, then pounded through the middle support.

Even as the pain began to numb the bones of my hand, the bookshelf began to topple.

"No!" I shouted hoarsely.

The bookshelf didn't listen. Like a tree surrendering to a lumberjack, it fell forward, gaining momentum with slow majesty.

The bookshelf smashed downward. Across the worktable. Across the almost-completed Spitfire. Model airplanes and model cars flew from the top and shattered against the far wall of the den.

It seemed like an earthquake, with aftershocks rumbling to a gradual silence, as my unbelieving eyes took in every detail of the destruction.

A slight whimper brought me back to reality.

It was Robbie. A single tear rolled down his cheek as he stood with bowed shoulders.

"I'm sorry," he said.

"Sorry?" I echoed. "Sorry?" I could feel frustration build again. Look what he'd done. And all he could say was sorry?

I raised my hand to point at him during the lecture I could feel ready to explode from me. I stopped as the sudden movement flashed pain through my hand.

Robbie misunderstood my silence and my upraised hand as a threat.

"Dad's gone and Mom's always busy," he said quickly as

he cringed. "I just wanted someone to talk to. And you're always helping your friends with homework. I thought if I made a list of questions, you would spend time with me. . . . " He bit his lip to keep from sobbing, and another tear trickled down his face. "You can hit me if you like. I won't duck. I deserve it."

The bones of the edge of my hand felt crushed. What would have happened to his face if I had actually connected? And all because I was the most important person in his life— so important he couldn't leave me alone. I flinched as I realized that the model airplane and a neat closet and perfect hair were more important to me than Robbie was.

I turned away so he couldn't see me blinking away the . . . the dust that must have come off the bookshelf and filled the air. I took a couple of deep breaths—not to control my anger but to find enough time to think of something that would put that shy, hopeful grin back on his face.

"Come on," I finally said. "Let's go outside and throw a baseball around."

His mouth dropped. "Really?"

"Yeah," I said. "What's more important, a tiny mess that can be cleaned up later, or you and me having fun when the sun is shining?"

I was almost glad for the way I had to wince each time I curled my hand around the baseball, because outside, Robbie's grin was as wide as his face and stayed as bright as the sun.

Still, that night I stared at the ceiling for long hours. Why *do* chalk erasers have stripes? Why *do* dogs have black lips? And, please, someone please tell me when fish sleep. . . .

WHAT'S UP THIS WEEK?

Sometimes lessons are learned the hard way. No news to anyone. John learns this firsthand when his work building a model airplane is lost because of his own impatience. Here's what's up for this week:

- Paying Attention to the Needs of Others
- Being like Christ
- Working toward Peace

PRAYER POWER

Take a minute to check with God. Ask him to help you recognize areas of selfishness in you, and expect him to show you what he wants you to learn this week.

TUESDAY

PAYING ATTENTION TO THE NEEDS OF OTHERS

Part of being unselfish involves paying attention to the needs of others. How do you balance your wants with the demands of others? Today's focus is all about that.

It's been said that we tend to hurt those closest to us. In some cases, that's our family. Other times it may be our friends. Let's take a closer look at John's attitudes and actions in "Dumb Brat."

BRAIN STRETCHERS
FOR KIDS:

1. How was John not thinking of Robbie, and what finally made him realize it?

2. When you were reading the story, could you understand John's feelings of frustration because of Robbie's questions? How do you think Robbie felt because of John's actions?

3. How do you think you would have reacted to Robbie? What would have been a better way for John to respond to his little brother? You may come up with several answers.

ASK AN ADULT:

1. Tell about a time when you acted selfishly toward y[ ]
kids. It may not be easy to admit this to them! But
admitting your own faults and mistakes is the first step
toward change for the better. What made you realize
you were being selfish, and what did you do about it?

SCRIPTURE POWER

We don't usually intentionally try to be selfish. It just seems
to happen. Sin is funny that way, kind of sneaking up on us.
The middle letter in the word *sin* is *i,* and at the center of
our sin is *I.* Through selfishness, we focus on what we want.
Kicking the selfishness habit begins with admitting the problem to God.

> Then Jesus said to the disciples, "If any of you wants to
> be my follower, you must put aside your selfish ambition,
> shoulder your cross, and follow me." (Matthew 16:24)

Part of following God is putting our own agendas in second
place—after God's plans and after thinking about other people. What's God's agenda? Love.

> Jesus replied, "The most important commandment is this:
> 'Hear, O Israel! The Lord our God is the one and only
> Lord. And you must love the Lord your God with all your
> heart, all your soul, all your mind, and all your strength.'
> The second is equally important: 'Love your neighbor as
> yourself.' No other commandment is greater than these."
> (Mark 12:29-31)

Well, okay, John probably knew he loved his little brother,
Robbie. But what was missing?

What does love look like? Let's take a look at what the apostle Paul wrote:

If I could speak in any language in heaven or on earth but didn't love others, I would only be making meaningless noise like a loud gong or a clanging cymbal. If I had the gift of prophecy, and if I knew all the mysteries of the future and knew everything about everything, but didn't love others, what good would I be? And if I had the gift of faith so that I could speak to a mountain and make it move, without love I would be no good to anybody. . . . Love is patient and kind. Love is not . . . rude. Love does not demand its own way. Love is not irritable, and it keeps no record of when it has been wronged. (1 Corinthians 13:1-2, 4-5)

PRAYER POWER

Take a minute or two to talk to God about ways you can be more unselfish. Ask him to develop his love in you and to help you make the effort to care about the interests of others.

BEING LIKE CHRIST

Yesterday we looked at the importance of thinking of others and loving them. Let's go a little deeper to find out more about being Christlike.

BRAIN STRETCHERS

FOR KIDS:

1. In what ways did John neglect to show Christ's love to Robbie?
2. How do you think Jesus would have reacted to Robbie's interruptions and questions?
3. In this week's story, what did John learn about his attitude?

ASK AN ADULT:

1. What does it mean to be Christlike?
2. Is it ever difficult for you to be Christlike?

SCRIPTURE POWER

Knowing God leads to self-control. Self-control leads to patient endurance, and patient endurance leads to godliness. (2 Peter 1:6)

There it is—the connection. Knowing God better results in more loving, less

selfish, actions toward the people in our life. Experiencing Christ's love makes us want to share that love!

> *Is there any encouragement from belonging to Christ? Any comfort from his love? Any fellowship together in the Spirit? Are your hearts tender and sympathetic? Then make me truly happy by agreeing wholeheartedly with each other, loving one another, and working together with one heart and purpose.*
> *(Philippians 2:1-2)*

When we are focused on how Christ treats us, it helps us to deal with other people more unselfishly. Jesus set the ultimate example for us. Like this week's Scripture says, even though Jesus was God, he gave up his position of power and became a man. He became a servant and died on a cross for sins he didn't commit! This great example of sacrifice and humility is one that we should copy.

PRAYER POWER

It's said that we become like the people we spend time with. That's very true in a relationship with Jesus. Talking to him and reading his Word are necessary if we're going to become more Christlike. So why not take a few minutes and ask God to help you become more like him? Praying is never wasted time!

WORKING TOWARD PEACE

Okay, so what's next? We've discussed thinking of others first and becoming more Christlike. The third element in this week's topic of unselfishness is working toward living at peace with others. That takes effort, and the willingness to work at it takes unselfishness.

BRAIN STRETCHERS

FOR KIDS:

1. In this week's story, what did John learn about his attitude?
2. Is it ever hard for you to live at peace with family and friends?

ASK AN ADULT:

1. How can you get to know God better?
2. How is God's peace helpful to you? Does it help you get along with others?

SCRIPTURE POWER

All of you should be of one mind, full of sympathy toward each other, loving one another with tender hearts and humble minds. (1 Peter 3:8)

Living in peace is difficult if we are focused on ourselves. It's easy to blame someone else when things are less than peaceful. Unselfish understanding is a key to living in peace. If we put ourselves in the other person's shoes, we may gain a new appreciation for the situation.

When you follow the desires of your sinful nature, your lives will produce these evil results: . . . hostility, quarreling, jealousy, outbursts of anger, selfish ambition, divisions. (Galatians 5:19-20)

There it is—the old sinful nature. It's at the center of selfishness, and it requires effort and strength from Jesus to overcome it.

PRAYER POWER

Only one more day this week. What do you want to say to God about unselfishness? about your efforts to live at peace with others? Maybe you've been having a tough time with that lately. Talk to God about it. He's waiting to hear from you.

CONCLUDING THOUGHTS

When things don't go our way, it's easy to lash out at others. It seems right to yell, get mad, or point out how wrong others are. What seems right and fair is often not truly right and fair. But God's way always is. So how can we learn to respond properly? The answer is to pray at all times. We don't need to dial long distance; God promises to meet us at our point of need. He'll give us the strength to do the right thing, if we're willing to ask.

In "Dumb Brat," John learned a valuable lesson from his annoying younger brother. It hit him over the head like a two-by-four, or maybe like a stack of falling books. John treated his friends with respect and was willing to help them, but he hadn't done the same for Robbie. Robbie noticed and came up with a way to get John's attention.

What do you think John learned? What lessons meant the most to you: paying attention to the needs of others? being like Christ? doing your part to work toward peace with others?

What did you learn about unselfishness this week?

LINE IT UP!

With your family or another small group, reenact the story as if John had responded unselfishly toward Robbie. Keep in mind that he needed to think about Robbie's need for attention, and he also needed to respond as Jesus would have. What specifically could John have said to work toward peace with his little brother? What would the results have been instead of toppling the shelves full of model airplanes? You can write out a script and assign roles: John, Robbie, and narrator. Have fun!

PRAYER POWER

Application time! Once more this week, talk to God about working on unselfishness in your life. Tell him what you learned, and spend a minute or two not talking. Just be quiet with God and listen for his voice to speak to you. He may not say something out loud, but he's sure to say something important to your heart.

WEEK 3

WHAT'S UP THIS WEEK:
Pride

THEME VERSE FOR THE WEEK:
Proverbs 29:23

Pride ends in humiliation, while humility brings
honor.

Sometimes those who appear to see the least really recognize the most. On a perfect winter day of snowboarding and showing off, Grant comes eye to eye with someone who sees far beyond what he has been used to looking at. Humility, being real, and finding self-worth in God are a few lessons he learns.

Show-Off

Okay. Say there's this girl you really want to impress. Say she's standing on the side of the ski hill, with silky black hair and a purple ski jacket. And say you're one of the best snowboarders on the entire hill.

Should be easy to impress her, right?

That's what I thought.

It was at the end of one of those perfect days on the ski hill. The air was clear and sharp, in the way that no one can understand unless they are actually on a mountain. Across the entire valley, and far away on the mountains on the other side, the spruce trees looked like green matchsticks. The sky was perfect blue with no clouds. Perfect white snow in all directions. Warm enough to be comfortable, but cold enough to make you feel really alive when you suck in a lungful of air.

And I was flying—I mean really *flying*—down the slope. I was hitting the bumps perfectly, catching plenty of air before landing. The edges of my snowboard crunched side to side in the tightly packed snow as I swished through the flat spots. Thirteen years old or not, I knew how to snowboard with the best of them.

Then, ahead of me, I saw her—soon enough to hit the brakes and send a spray of snow that covered her skis as I stopped beside her.

"Hello," I said. I've never been shy. I don't have to be.

She turned her face toward me. She smiled beneath her dark ski goggles. The sun caught her dark hair where it streamed out from the strap of her goggles. My heart did a little flip.

"Hello?" By her voice, *she* sounded shy.

"Grant's my name," I said. I grinned. Since people think I'm cute, it was a good grin to flash. Especially now. "Snowboarding's my game."

It was a dumb thing to say. But it always made people smile.

She smiled. "My name is Allie."

I guessed she was about my age. I wanted to ask a million questions. What school did she go to? What was her favorite music? How much did she like me already?

So I asked my first question. "Want to ski with me? I can show you the best runs."

"Maybe not," she said. "I usually don't—"

"Come on," I said. "Ski with me, that's where you want to be."

People skied past us. The hill was not too crowded.

Enough room for me to show off without hitting anyone, and enough skiers around that it was worthwhile to show off.

"Come on," I tried again. "Make a run. You'll find it fun."

She leaned against her ski poles. She shook her head.

"It might not be a good idea," she said.

"What?" I grinned again. "I'm the best. Just ignore the rest."

Allie grinned back. "You're funny. Like Dr. Seuss."

"That's nothing," I said. "Watch this."

I pushed off. Seconds later, I hit a jump and spun a complete circle in the air. Off the next jump, I spun a circle and a half, landing backwards.

"Oooh," I heard someone say. "Did you see Grant hit that awesome 540?"

I leaned way back on my snowboard until the nose of it tilted into the air. I grabbed the nose of it with my hand and rode it like someone doing a wheelie on a bicycle.

A second later, I hit another jump and got at least five feet of air. While still in the air, I kicked my heels upward so that the snowboard was almost as high as my waist. I grabbed the board with my hand, and just before landing, I let go again.

Finally, I stopped—100 yards down the hill from where she still leaned against her poles.

If that bunch of tricks hadn't impressed her, nothing would.

I waited for her to ski down and join me.

She didn't.

That gave me two choices: Ski out the rest of this run, take the chairlift to the top, and ski down to her, or climb up from where I was.

I decided if I took the chairlift, I might not find her again.

I stepped out of my snowboard and began to climb. It took five hard minutes to reach her.

"Hey!" I said.

"Grant?" Allie turned her face toward me.

I pretended I was hurt. "Forgotten me already?"

"No, but—"

"I did the tricks," I said. "It give you kicks?"

She laughed. "Who are you?"

"I told you already. Grant's the name. Snowboarding's the game."

"Seriously. It's like you're not afraid of anything. Who are you?"

"Find out by spending time with me," I said. I looked right into her eyes. Or at least the dark ski goggles that covered her eyes. "In less than an hour, they close down the hill for the day. We can meet tomorrow and ski. What do you say?"

"I'm sorry," she said. "Tomorrow is Sunday. I go to church with my parents and then we spend the rest of the day visiting my grandparents."

"Church, smurch," I said. "I can teach you all the cool tricks. Didn't you see? Weren't they good enough?"

"Well . . ."

"Watch," I said. "I'll do a fakie and some killer loops."

I pushed off again. This time I really outdid myself. I did a fakie, riding backwards. Then I hit those killer loops like I promised, jumping high. On one of them, I did a full somersault in the air. It nearly killed me, but I landed right and kept on going.

Other people applauded.

She didn't. Allie stayed right where she was, leaning against her ski poles.

Again, I had to climb all the way back up to her.

"Hey!" I said again.

"Grant." This time, at least, she didn't ask it like a question.

"Listen," I said. "This is wearing me out. What do I have to do to get you to ski with me tomorrow?"

"I told you," Allie said. She smiled. "Tomorrow is Sunday and—"

"I know. Church."

"You could always go with me and my parents," Allie said.

"I hardly know you!" Skiing with a pretty girl was one thing. But making a big step like going to church was another. "Besides, church is for sissies."

"Sissies?"

"You know." I grinned. "Like girls who won't ski all the cool runs with me."

She smiled and took it like the joke I meant it to be.

Then she got serious. "Let me tell you," she said. "What I learned in church is what gives me courage. It wasn't a sissy who died on the cross for me."

Serious as her words were, she kept smiling, so it didn't feel like she was lecturing me.

"Anyway," she said, "because of him, I'm not as scared about a lot of things as I used to be."

It was pretty serious. I needed a joke to loosen things up. "So maybe Monday you'll hit those cool runs with me?"

"I can't," she said. "I'm blind."

Blind? The shock hit me hard, and it felt like minutes were passing on the clock as my mind struggled to grasp her words.

Then I understood. Her dark goggles. The way she turned her face to my voice. Why she hadn't skied down the hill to join me. Why she hadn't recognized me when I climbed back up to her. And why my tricks hadn't impressed her.

Blind. She had way more courage than I did.

"Wow," I said. "And you still ski."

43

"It's not a big deal," she said. "I go slow. And my dad always stays nearby."

"I don't see him," I said.

"Neither do I," Allie said. She waited. "Get it? I was making a joke."

I laughed. This was a remarkable girl.

"When I ski, Dad stays with me," she said. "He asked me to wait here while he made a run of his own. He'll be back any second."

"Oh," I said.

Then I realized something else. Allie had asked me to go to church with her. Not because I was a good snowboarder who impressed her and not because she thought I was cute (she couldn't see if I was or not) but because she liked who I was.

It was a nice thought. She liked me for who I was, not for what I was trying to be.

"About this church thing," I said. "What do you say I give it a fling?"

WHAT'S UP THIS WEEK?

- Arrogance and Humility
- Finding Self-Worth in God
- Being Real

PRAYER POWER

Preparing our hearts to accept what God has to say is an important part of growing closer to him. Ask him what he wants you to see this week, and ask him to help you see yourself in the same way he sees you.

ARROGANCE AND HUMILITY

Arrogance and pride are very similar traits. When we think too highly of ourselves, we tend to be less humble and more tempted to brag and act like big stuff around others. When we do that, though, we aren't letting people see who we really are.

BRAIN STRETCHERS
FOR KIDS:

1. What evidence is there that Grant was proud and even cocky? Pick out specific lines from the story that made you realize this.
2. What was it about Allie's actions toward him that made Grant realize she liked him for more important reasons than what he looked like or how well he could snowboard?
3. It's important to have confidence. But how do you know Grant was too confident or proud?

ASK AN ADULT:

1. With your family, think through some of the differences between confidence and pride.

2. Can you think of a time when you were too confident and fell flat on your face? Tell what you learned.

SCRIPTURE POWER

Pride goes before destruction, and haughtiness before a fall. (Proverbs 16:18)

Being too proud ruins us! That doesn't mean we can't feel good about our accomplishments—it is good to work at doing something well, and we should feel great when we excel in an area of our lives. The kind of pride spoken of in Proverbs 16 has to do with taking the credit for our abilities rather than using them to praise God. Grant was consumed with his own greatness rather than with God's.

The arrogance of all people will be brought low. Their pride will lie in the dust. The Lord alone will be exalted! (Isaiah 2:17)

Arrogance is another word for too much pride. The Bible gets pretty specific about God's view of arrogance. He deserves our praise and the credit for our accomplishments. And he's not thrilled when we take the credit he deserves for the abilities he's given us. Check out this next verse to see just how serious God is about pride:

I will crush the arrogance of the proud and the haughtiness of the mighty. (Isaiah 13:11)

It's pretty clear: God won't share his glory with us! And we shouldn't expect him to.

PRAYER POWER

Pride is a serious thing. It's easy for it to sneak up on us gradually. A great accomplishment on the athletic field, an awesome grade on a test, or scoring big on the popularity scale—all are memorable moments. But pray this week that God will show you ways that pride may creep into your heart. Ask him to help you take pride in the abilities he's given you without taking the credit he deserves.

WEDNESDAY

FINDING SELF-WORTH IN GOD

Yesterday we discovered some truths about pride. Now we've gotten the idea that we shouldn't take credit for the abilities God gave us. So just how should we balance feeling good about ourselves without getting cocky? The answer comes in finding our self-esteem in God. Today let's find out what that means.

BRAIN STRETCHERS

FOR KIDS:

1. What abilities or qualities about himself did Grant usually use to impress people?
2. Was Allie confident, or was she cocky? Back up your answer with phrases from the story.
3. Who really had more courage, Grant or Allie? What did Grant learn from Allie?
4. What gave Allie her courage and confidence?

ASK AN ADULT:

1. What is important about having a good sense of self-worth?

2. How does knowing that God loves you give you a better view of yourself?

SCRIPTURE POWER

Be on guard. Stand true to what you believe. Be coura-geous. Be strong. (1 Corinthians 16:13)

It's tough to be courageous and to stand up for your beliefs if you don't feel good about yourself. Allie might not have felt too great about being blind. She could have let that affect her self-esteem. But she didn't. Instead, she focused on God. She knew God loved her, so she didn't feel a need to impress other people, including Grant. God's love for her made her strong and gave her courage. His love can do the same for any of us.

We put no confidence in human effort. Instead, we boast about what Christ Jesus has done for us. Yet I could have confidence in myself if anyone could. If others have reason for confidence in their own efforts, I have even more! (Philippians 3:3-4)

Yes, there is a good kind of confidence! The apostle Paul wrote those verses to explain just where our confidence should come from: Jesus Christ. We'd all be in pretty bad shape if he hadn't chosen to die for our sins. Our life is noth-ing without him. When things are going well, we have a tendency to think it is because of how great we are. We need to be reminded to give God the praise for everything good in our life, remembering that our gifts and abilities come from him. As Christians, we should have a healthy amount of confidence and self-esteem. After all, the king of the universe knows and loves us perfectly. That's no small deal. But the center of our confidence needs to rest in Christ.

PRAYER POWER

Has anything in this week's theme hit home for you? Pride and confidence are topics that most of us need to work on. Sometimes we have too much and we get cocky; other times we need to improve our self-esteem. Talk to God about where you are in this area. Confess areas of too much pride, and ask him to increase your courage in the areas where he knows you need improvement.

BEING REAL

In our theme of pride this week, we've talked about humility and getting our confidence and self-worth from God instead of from our accomplishments. Now let's discuss what the results will be if we apply these lessons. When our pride is under control and our confidence comes from knowing who we are in Christ, we have the ability to be real. That's the focus of today's study. Let's begin with this question: Who acted with the freedom to be real, Grant or Allie?

BRAIN STRETCHERS

FOR KIDS:

1. What abilities do you have that you tend to be proud of in a way that might be displeasing to God?
2. What do you think it means to be real?

ASK AN ADULT:

1. Have you ever been in a situation where you've tried to act in a way that really doesn't show your true personality?
2. Why is pride such a downfall for Christians?

SCRIPTURE POWER

People judge by outward appearance, but the Lord looks at a person's thoughts and intentions. (1 Samuel 16:7)

Have you noticed how important appearances are to some people? In all honesty, each of us probably falls into the pattern of putting too much emphasis on image. When we're too concerned about our own coolness, we tend to overlook the qualities that truly matter. This often brings a false confidence, known as pride. And when we're being false, obviously we're not being real.

So we are always confident, even though we know that as long as we live in these bodies we are not at home with the Lord. That is why we live by believing and not by seeing. . . . So our aim is to please him always, whether we are here in this body or away from this body. . . . It is because we know this solemn fear of the Lord that we work so hard to persuade others. God knows we are sincere, and I hope you know this, too. Are we trying to pat ourselves on the back again? No, we are giving you a reason to be proud of us, so you can answer those who brag about having a spectacular ministry rather than having a sincere heart before God. . . . Whatever we do, it is because Christ's love controls us. Since we believe that Christ died for everyone, we also believe that we have all died to the old life we used to live. He died for everyone so that those who receive his new life will no longer live to please themselves. Instead, they will live to please Christ, who died and was raised for them. (2 Corinthians 5:6-15)

Whoa. Okay, let's digest this. What does it all mea[n]
was looking at his abilities through his own eyes—
was quite impressed. But his focus on his image
from valuing what was real and important. Allie
even see his accomplishments, yet she saw so much more.
She saw an opportunity to share Christ's love with Grant.
Her confidence had everything to do with her sincere desire
to show God's love to Grant. Her actions showed a genuine-
ness that attracted Grant. She was real.

PRAYER POWER
One more day this week. Spend a little time talking to God
about areas of pride in your heart. What things have come
to mind over the week? Have you noticed yourself thinking
about these lessons when you've been tempted to feel too
proud? We've all been there! Ask God to help you balance
feeling good about yourself with not becoming cocky.

CONCLUDING THOUGHTS

Not everything is exactly as it seems.

Have you ever looked at a hologram—you know, one of those pictures where you can see one image from one angle, and then a different image appears from another angle? People can sometimes be like holograms. You look at them a certain way, thinking that you have them figured out, when suddenly you see another side to them that you hadn't expected.

In "Show-Off," there were two sides to Grant: the outward pride he showed because of his snowboarding abilities, and the real personality inside. He was an awesome snowboarder and he knew it. When he saw a good-looking girl on the ski slopes, he decided to impress her with his talent, charm, and good looks. But Allie wasn't all that impressed by his spins, jumps, and board-grabs—or his good looks—because she couldn't see him!

Yet Allie's faith in God helped her see much more. And her healthy self-worth that came from knowing God's love for her gave her courage to take a stand about going to church on Sunday rather than skiing with Grant. She did not make excuses about her faith. As a result, Grant respected her and decided to give church a chance.

Pride gets in the way of your ability to be your true self. It's a sign that you're putting too much focus on your accomplishments and the things you *do* instead of who you *are.* Knowing who you are to Jesus gives you the right perspective and helps you have confidence without being too proud.

Are there areas of pride you need to work on?

LINE IT UP!

Spend some time thinking about all the abilities God has given you. Maybe you're a great musician or athlete. Maybe you're a good listener or you get straight A's. Being confident because of those abilities is great; being too proud and using them to cover up who you really are isn't good. Go ahead and write down all the talents you can think of. It's good to think positively about your talents and accomplishments. At the end of the list, write a prayer to God to thank him for giving you those abilities. Then finish the prayer by writing about how you're going to give him the credit instead of keeping it for yourself.

PRAYER POWER

Spend a few minutes praying through the issue of pride. Ask God to help you remember this week's lesson whenever you're tempted to be too proud of things you've done. Ask him to give you a right attitude about your accomplishments.

WEEK 4

WHAT'S UP THIS WEEK:
Forgiveness

THEME VERSES FOR THE WEEK:
Luke 15:11-32

Jesus told them this story: "A man had two sons. The younger son told his father, 'I want my share of your estate now, instead of waiting until you die.' So his father agreed to divide his wealth between his sons. A few days later this younger son packed all his belongings and took a trip to a distant land, and there he wasted all his money on wild living. . . . When he finally came to his senses . . . he returned home to his father. And while he was still a long distance away, his father saw him coming. Filled with love and compassion, he ran to his son, embraced him, and kissed him. His son said to him, 'Father, I have sinned against both heaven and you, and I am no longer worthy of being called your son.'

But his father said to the servants, 'Quick! Bring the finest robe in the house and put it on him. Get a ring for his finger, and sandals for his feet. And kill the calf we have been fattening in the pen. We must celebrate with a feast, for this son of mine was dead and has now returned to life. He was lost, but now he is found.' So the party began. Meanwhile, the older son was in the fields working. When he returned home, he . . . was angry and wouldn't go in. His father came out and begged him, but he replied, 'All these years I've worked hard for you and never once refused to do a single thing you told me to. And in all that time you never gave me even one young goat for a feast with my friends. Yet when this son of yours comes back after squandering your money . . . you celebrate by killing the finest calf we have.' His father said to him, 'Look, dear son, you and I are very close, and everything I have is yours. We had to celebrate this happy day. For your brother was dead and has come back to life! He was lost, but now he is found!' "

When his older brother, Josh, returns home after wasting his parents' money and causing a ton of hurt to his family, Caleb naturally has some mixed feelings about all the attention and forgiveness his parents give Josh. Sometimes life doesn't seem fair. But God's definition of forgiveness is so much more than fair.

A Small Wooden Cross

I heard it halfway through my paper route, from gray-haired Mr. Chambers as he watered his rosebushes: My brother Josh was back. That's the kind of town we live in. News travels fast. And standing there on the sidewalk, as Mr. Chambers stared down his nose at me through his bifocals, waiting for my reaction, I knew exactly what I would do: punch Josh in the nose. That was only the beginning of what he deserved.

I can't remember if I said that out loud to Mr. Chambers or if I was just thinking it real loud in my head. Either way, I left Mr. Chambers behind and stomped toward my house. My newspaper bag flapped at my side, reminding me of the 20 papers I still had to deliver before dark. But I didn't care. For once, the papers could wait.

I was only three blocks from home. That distance covers about half the size of our town, which is set in the middle of the Texas plains. American flag in front of the courthouse, high school football on Friday nights, and everybody in church on Sundays. Josh always called our town boring. I call it steady and safe.

As I walked, I ignored the warm evening breeze against my face. I shut out the music of the bugs. I didn't even wave at the McCluskey twins, sitting on their front porch sipping lemonade.

What filled my mind were thoughts of how good it would feel to pop my brother in the nose. Sure, I was six years younger. But I had justice on my side. Plus, I was big for a 13-year-old—one of the toughest in my class. I had a crew cut and played football. Josh was longhaired and played guitar.

As I got closer to the house, I smelled barbeque, which was strange. Only a week past Easter, it was early in the season for a barbeque, even during this spell of good weather. Even stranger, I soon saw that the barbeque was set up in my backyard. There was my dad, his big, strong face showing a grin above the fence as he laughed with some neighbors standing beside him. I couldn't remember the last time I'd seen my dad laughing. Which alone was a good enough reason for popping my brother in the nose.

I dropped my newspaper bag on the front porch instead of hanging it up in the usual place in the usual responsible way.

"I'm home!" I said as I walked inside the house. Music— an old Beach Boys cassette—was playing so loud I had to yell. I couldn't remember the last time I'd heard my mom singing along with the Beach Boys. Another reason to pop my longhaired brother.

Mom stepped into the hallway from the kitchen. Her hands were covered with flour dust.

"Caleb," she said, "Josh is back!"

"I know," I said. "Mr. Chambers told me."

"You'll find Josh in his bedroom," she said. "But don't spend too much time with him up there. Food will be ready in about half an hour and we want you both down for the celebration."

She held up her hands, showing me the flour dust up to her wrists. "I'm just getting ready to put a cherry pie in the oven. Josh's favorite. Make sure you're washed up, all right?"

"Sure," I said. What she didn't know was that I intended to wash Josh's blood off my knuckles.

I marched up the stairs. Josh's bedroom door was closed like it had been for the last six months. Only tonight he was on the other side of it, instead of causing my parents pain from somewhere in California.

I almost pushed his door open right then, but I decided I needed something from my bedroom first. My journal.

It was on top of my desk, beside the math homework I had finished before going out to deliver my newspapers. I grabbed the journal, spun around, and headed back to Josh's room.

"Hey," he said from the edge of his bed as I pushed his door open. "It's good to see you, Caleb. Real good."

For a second, I couldn't get any words out of my mouth. The first surprise was how easy it would be to pop him. He seemed about half the size he'd been before leaving town a year earlier. His shoulders were shrunken. The gray skin of

61

his face was tight on his cheekbones. His hair was dull and greasy and much longer than I remembered.

The second surprise was the Dallas Cowboys jersey he wore. It was the Dallas Cowboys jersey Dad had promised me for getting all A's on my report card.

"Give me a hug," Josh said. "It's good to be home."

Josh stood and held his arms out.

I put my hand against his knobby chest and pushed him back onto the bed.

"Funny," I told him. "I never heard any of your songs on the radio. Like maybe you never became a rock star."

"Long story," he said. "Real long story. Let me tell you, it was a lesson about dreams. I mean—"

"Long story?" I flipped open my journal. "Let *me* read *you* a long story. I'm the one who had to watch Mom and Dad suffer. I've been keeping a diary just so you'd know this stuff when you got back."

I scanned my handwriting. "Let's see. April 15. No good-bye from Josh. No word on where he went. Mom has spent three days crying on the couch. Dad still hasn't gotten things figured out with the banker. The lawyer, though, says Josh could take all his trust-fund money once he turned 18."

"Caleb—"

"No," I said. "You listen to me."

I flipped through the journal. "May 2. Our first postcard from Josh. Santa Monica. He's living in a beach house on the ocean. The neighbors gossip that a month on the beach costs the same as a year's tuition at university. Mom says Grandpa would be rolling over in his grave to discover what's hap-pened to the money from the sale of his ranch."

"I know it was stupid," Josh said. "But I had all these"

songs in my head. There was Grandpa's will. And a town like this isn't the place to—"

"June 14," I read from another page. "A call from the police in Hollywood. Would we post bail for a Joshua Heppner of no fixed address? June 15. Dad flies out to Los Angeles. June 16. Dad flies back. No Joshua. Mom cries for another week."

"I thought I just needed another two months," Josh said. "I was sure the big break was just around the corner. Dad was going to take me away. I had to find a way to ditch him. And my friends wanted to party."

"August 23," I said through tight lips. "Collect phone call from Josh at 4:00 A.M. from the Los Angeles General Hospital. Dad flies out again. Flies home again. No Joshua. Josh had run from the hospital, leaving Dad to pay when he got there."

I snapped the journal shut. "Then nothing more from you. Mom and Dad thought you were dead. I could tell you about the gossip, the neighbors, and how I had to do all the work around the store because Mom was depressed. I could tell you about the money Dad had to borrow from my college savings to pay for your hospital bill. But I'll bet you wouldn't care, would you?"

Josh looked down at the floor.

"And on top of all that, now you're wearing my Dallas Cowboys jersey."

"My clothes were pretty ripped up," Josh said, without bringing his eyes to mine. "It took five days to hitchhike here. I didn't have money for food, let alone new clothes. Dad said he'd get you a jersey tomorrow."

"Stand up," I told him. "Stand up so I can pop you."

He stood. "I deserve whatever you give me. My money ran

63

out. My friends left me. All their promises to get my songs on the radio were just an excuse for them to spend my money. All I wanted was to be with my family again, even if it took living in a doghouse in the backyard."

He smiled. A front tooth was missing. "Hit me as hard as you want. I won't cry. I did enough of that on the way here—in truck stops and ditches. It was a long haul since Easter Sunday."

I brought my fist back. "Easter? Mom cried too. She kept praying for you to call collect so she'd know you were still alive."

"Before you hit me," he said, "let me give you one thing—the thing that brought me home."

He reached around his neck and pulled a thin silver chain over his head. It got stuck in his hair. He had to tug until it was finally loose. The chain held a small wooden cross.

"You gave this to me when you were nine years old," he said. "You might not even remember. It was a Sunday school thing you made during a lesson on forgiveness. You gave it to me because I had broken one of your toys and you wanted me to know it was all right."

I looked at the cross. I remembered giving it to my brother back when I adored him.

"This cross was all I had left in California," he said. "Things were so bad I was digging food out of garbage cans. I woke up Easter Sunday in an alley with the cross digging into my neck. It made me think of church again. So I went to a downtown mission and listened to a bearded preacher tell me that Jesus had died to save me from my sins—that because of Jesus, I could go home to heaven, no matter what I had done."

Josh put his hand on my shoulder. "His forgiveness was my

only hope, Caleb. And forgiveness is nothing a person can ever earn. They can only give it or accept it."

With his other hand, Josh gently opened the fist I still held high, ready to punch into his nose. Josh closed my fingers around the small wooden cross and spoke softly. "So I came home, hoping you and Mom and Dad might give me something I didn't deserve. . . . "

Josh stepped away. He opened the door and closed it behind him. He left me alone in his bedroom. Fist clenched around the cross. Staring at the wall.

I could tell you I forgave him. Or I could tell you I left the house in anger because Mom and Dad had welcomed him back with open arms.

But I don't want to tell you what I did after I left his bedroom. Because I'm wondering what you would do if you were me and Josh was your brother. Would you go downstairs and celebrate because he finally came home after a long time lost? Or would you stay mad and hateful because he got the treatment you thought you deserved?

If you really push me for the answer, though, I'll give you the same peaceful smile that Josh gave me just before stepping out of the bedroom to leave me alone with my thoughts. And if you still push me to find out, I'll tell you only one other thing: The answer is in the cross. . . .

WHAT'S UP THIS WEEK?

Caleb's feelings about the situation being unfair seem pretty reasonable, right? His brother messed up big time, and he should pay, right? Wrong. Obviously, Caleb learned a greater lesson. Let's dig in deeper and learn some stuff about the whole idea of forgiveness. Here's how we'll break it up:

65

- When Life Seems Unfair
- Admitting to Self-Righteousness
- Letting Go of Grudges

PRAYER POWER

Forgiveness is a tough topic, especially when life seems unfair and the good guys don't seem to win all the time. Take a few minutes to think about situations in your life that need forgiveness and that you need to talk about with God. Ask yourself whether your heart is really open to hearing the truth from God. Then pray—and listen to what God has to tell you.

WHEN LIFE SEEMS UNFAIR

It's happened to all of us: Someone gets something we want, and we feel like we've missed out. It's frustrating! Especially when it seems we're more deserving. Those can be tough situations, making it seem impossible to forgive a person. But what should our response be?

BRAIN STRETCHERS

FOR KIDS:

1. Can you think of a time when someone else got something you deserved? What about a time when you got something you didn't deserve? How did you feel?

2. In "A Small Wooden Cross," there was nothing Josh could do to make up for his mistakes. There is nothing any of us can do to make up for our sin either. How does that make you feel?

ASK AN ADULT:

1. We've learned some stuff about God's amazing grace. What is grace? Is it something we earn?

How has God shown us grace? (Hint: Look up Hebrews 2:9.)

2. How about spending some time talking about what Jesus did when he paid the price for our sin? Are we supposed to follow Jesus' example of forgiveness when something isn't fair?

SCRIPTURE POWER

Love is not irritable, and it keeps no record of when it has been wronged. (1 Corinthians 13:5)

Sometimes life isn't fair. Things aren't always divided up evenly, and we don't like it when we aren't getting what we feel we have coming to us. But we can't afford to spend our life trying to make sure everything is fair. We'll just end up frustrated, and we'll spend all of our energy attempting to split up life's jelly beans evenly and struggling to get our portion. The Bible says love doesn't do that; it doesn't keep a record.

Jesus came to take away our sins, for there is no sin in him. (1 John 3:5)

Jesus didn't deserve to die, but he did it willingly, taking our sin on himself. Talk about unfair! He took the whole world's sin, because he knew it was the only way that we could be in a right place with God. We couldn't earn salvation, but God made a way for us to be right with him—by accepting his gift. God making it possible for us to have salvation should change the way we think about justice and fairness.

Your decrees are always fair; help me to understand them, that I may live. (Psalm 119:144)

Fortunately, God is always fair. What good news! Somehow in the big scheme of things, he'll make everything right for each of us when we handle things his way. That's part of his grace. It covers unfairness.

PRAYER POWER

As you pray today, ask God to help you recognize when you feel like griping because of unfairness. Wrong attitudes can creep into our mind so easily, and many times they come from feeling like we've been treated unfairly. Ask God to help you see how the love and mercy he shows you can help you show the same things to others.

ADMITTING TO SELF-RIGHTEOUSNESS

Caleb's story is very similar to the older brother's story in this week's theme Scripture passage. Both of them felt overlooked and cheated out of being recognized for doing what was right. What they didn't realize was that an attitude of self-righteousness—overlooking their own sin by focusing too much on someone else's—was messing them up. Self-righteousness gets in the way of forgiveness.

BRAIN STRETCHERS
FOR KIDS:

1. How would you have responded if you were Caleb in "A Small Wooden Cross"? Do you think you would have had some of the same angry, unforgiving feelings toward Josh?

2. Has there been a time when you've struggled to forgive someone because he or she didn't deserve it? What do you think God wants you to do in situations like that?

ASK AN ADULT:
1. Sometimes people say someone is "holier than thou." What does that mean?
2. Okay, now it's your turn to tell how you would have responded to Josh if you were in Caleb's shoes.
3. Has there ever been a time when you've felt self-righteous and didn't want to forgive someone? What did you do?

SCRIPTURE POWER

Why worry about a speck in your friend's eye when you have a log in your own? How can you think of saying, "Friend, let me help you get rid of that speck in your eye," when you can't see past the log in your own eye? Hypocrite! First get rid of the log from your own eye; then perhaps you will see well enough to deal with the speck in your friend's eye. (Luke 6:41-42)

Because Caleb was focusing so much on what Josh had done wrong, he didn't notice his own unforgiving attitude. Oops. That's an easy mistake to make, but it's one that can be very hurtful to others. It's the sin of self-righteousness.

We love each other as a result of his loving us first. (1 John 4:19)

With self-righteousness, just as with unfairness, God sets the example for us to follow. We continue to cause him pain because we continue to be imperfect people who sin. Yet he is always willing to let go of his right to stay angry at us. That is real love! And he asks us to follow his lead and act like him. Here's more:

71

God blesses those who are merciful, for they will be shown mercy. (Matthew 5:7)

Stop judging others, and you will not be judged. For others will treat you as you treat them. Whatever measure you use in judging others, it will be used to measure how you are judged. (Matthew 7:1-2)

When we do dumb things, we hope people will forgive us and give us another chance. When others do things that hurt us, however, it can be very difficult for us to forgive them and extend them grace. God's love and mercy toward us are our examples and reminders to forgive others, even when we've been treated unfairly. Jesus paid the ultimate price to forgive our unfairness to him. He doesn't ask us to do any more than what he did.

PRAYER POWER

It's time to pray about this. Self-righteousness can be a very sneaky sin. We often don't recognize it in ourselves until it hurts someone else and is pointed out to us. Spend some time asking God to show you areas of self-righteousness and judgment in you that are getting in the way of a forgiving spirit.

LETTING GO OF GRUDGES

We've spent time discussing forgiveness when things don't seem fair. And we've learned some things about recognizing self-righteousness. Now it's time to deal honestly with the hard reality that forgiving others can be incredibly tough. Sometimes hanging on to a grudge seems so much better. So then what do you do?

BRAIN STRETCHERS

FOR KIDS:

1. What does it mean to hold a grudge? Does it feel good sometimes to stay angry at someone?
2. Have you ever held a grudge? Have you let go of it yet?

ASK AN ADULT:

1. What makes it so hard to let go of a grudge? Do adults struggle with this too?
2. What's wrong with staying angry? Does it hurt the person holding a grudge?

SCRIPTURE POWER

If you forgive those who sin against you, your heavenly Father will forgive you. But if you refuse to forgive others, your Father will not forgive your sins. (Matthew 6:14-15)

This is what the Lord says: O Israel, my faithless people, come home to me again, for I am merciful. I will not be angry with you forever. Only acknowledge your guilt. Admit that you rebelled against the Lord your God. (Jeremiah 3:12-13)

So whenever you speak, or whatever you do, remember that you will be judged by the law of love, the law that set you free. For there will be no mercy for you if you have not been merciful to others. But if you have been merciful, then God's mercy toward you will win out over his judgment against you. (James 2:12-13)

We know God commands us to forgive others. He even puts an ultimatum on the command. We can't expect to be treated better than we're willing to treat others. Where does the strength—or even just the desire—to forgive come from? You guessed it. It all comes from God.

Instead, be kind to each other, tenderhearted, forgiving one another, just as God through Christ has forgiven you. (Ephesians 4:32)

Think for a minute about how much God is willing to forgive us. Really let it sink in. The price Jesus paid to forgive us was deadly; it couldn't have cost him more. He hates sin, and we were full of it. But did he hold a grudge? Nope. Thankfully,

God didn't give up on us but was willing to sacrifice greatly to forgive us. Makes a person think, huh?

PRAYER POWER

What thoughts have gone through your mind during this week's study? What are your thoughts toward God about his forgiveness for you? Thankfulness? Awe? Tell him.

CONCLUDING THOUGHTS

In "A Small Wooden Cross," Caleb wanted to punch Josh in the nose, and Josh deserved it. Josh had wasted the money his grandparents and parents had worked hard for years to save. Even worse, he had caused his family months of heartache and grief. And then he had the nerve to show up at home again after all the pain he'd caused.

Caleb understood forgiveness. It was the message he relayed to Josh when he gave him the cross necklace at nine years old. Caleb just needed to be reminded of what forgiveness is all about. The old wooden cross was that reminder for him. The old wooden cross should be a reminder for us all.

Just like Josh, one of the sons in this week's theme Scripture passage took his father's money and left the family. It's tough to see someone do stupid things, and it's even tougher to forgive them and accept them back after they do it, especially when we've been hurt in the process.

But heaven rejoices when a sinner returns to God in repentance. God doesn't look at us with a frown on his face and demand that we try to make up for our sin. That's a very good thing! We could never pay the price. God is so happy to have us back, and he forgives us completely—so completely, in fact, that he fully erases the sin from his mind and doesn't remember it anymore.

So what are you going to do next time it's tempting to be unforgiving because things seem unfair, because you feel you have a right to your self-righteousness, or because you don't want to let go of a grudge?

LINE IT UP!

Is there a situation you're dealing with now or have been faced with in the past where it's been tough to forgive? Sometimes it helps to get your thoughts on paper. Writing out our feelings can do a lot to help us see things realistically and can even open our eyes to our own fault in a situation. Holding on to a grudge will hurt you more than it hurts the person with whom you're angry. So why not take a few minutes and write a journal entry or a letter to the person who has made you angry? Spill your guts; vent; get it all out! Then toss the paper as a sign that you're purposely choosing to forgive and let go. Or, if you really need to share your feelings with the person, pray about sending the letter to him or her. Just keep in mind that your words will either hurt the person or work toward fixing the relationship. Motivation matters to God, so it's important to make sure the words you share with that person are ones that are not full of anger.

PRAYER POWER

Take time to do more than just spit out a few sentences to God about this week's topic of forgiveness. An unforgiving spirit can destroy you if you don't deal with it. It hurts you at least as much as it hurts others. We dug in to God's Word this week and saw just a few of the times God addressed this issue. It's nothing to mess with. So talk to him about it. Ask him to work in your heart. He'll even give you the desire to forgive. He'll meet you where you are. Just go to him.

WHAT'S UP THIS WEEK:
A Consistent Christian

THEME VERSES FOR THE WEEK:
James 2:14; 3:13

Dear brothers and sisters, what's the use of
saying you have faith if you don't prove it by
your actions? That kind of faith can't save anyone. . . . If you are wise and understand God's
ways, live a life of steady goodness so that only
good deeds will pour forth. And if you don't
brag about the good you do, then you will be
truly wise!

Joey is about to learn something important about being a Christian: consistency. He's known for breaking the rules and getting away with it. As you read about him, ask yourself what you would do in his place.

A Hassrock Classic

As I tried to skate between the defenseman and the boards, I saw his elbow coming. But I couldn't duck it. *Boom!* Right in the cheekbone. I slid to the ice, grateful for the hockey gear that protected me.

From the stands, the crowd roared in anger. Then I heard what I'd been waiting for. The referee's whistle, stopping the play.

The defenseman for the Thunderbirds was about to get a two-minute penalty. It meant he'd have to sit out, giving us a big one-man advantage until we scored a goal or his penalty expired.

I rolled on the ice as if he'd really hurt me. It didn't hurt to try to get sympathy from the referee. As I rolled, I did one other thing, which really *did* hurt me. I bit the inside of my cheek. Hard. Until I tasted blood.

I got up. Guys on my team were skating in close to see if I was okay.

I leaned over and spit blood onto the ice, then looked up to see if the referee had noticed.

He did. He raised his arm and pointed at the Thunderbird defenseman. "Five-minute major," the ref barked. "Get to the penalty box."

I hid my grin until I had skated over to the players' box and the rest of my team.

"You all right?" Franky, our trainer, asked.

I grinned at the guys. "A Hassrock Classic, boys. All I had to do was show a little blood, and voilà, a five-minute penalty instead of a two-minute one! Go out there and get a goal."

Franky rolled his eyes. The hockey season was less than a month old, and *Hassrock Classic* was itself already a classic phrase. It covered all of my tricks on the ice. If anyone wanted lessons in how to break the rules and not get caught, I was the one to watch.

On the ice? If someone clutches at you while you've got the puck, make sure you fall in a big, dramatic dive. It gets the other team a penalty. That's a Hassrock Classic. Or hang on to a guy's jersey when the ref isn't looking, and let the guy drag you along, slowing him down and speeding you up. The best one? When you know a guy on the other team is getting a penalty for elbowing you, bite the inside of your mouth real hard and start spitting out blood and pretend you're hurt real bad. It gives him an automatic five-minute major penalty, instead of just a two-minute minor penalty. That's a Hassrock Classic.

"Yup," Franky said. "A Hassrock Classic. Hey, kid—you are a beaut, Joey. Every trick in the book. Good thing you go to church every Sunday. Gives you a chance to pray hard over the things you do the rest of the week!"

I grinned back, but inside I was angry. Sure, I was a Christian and went to church. But I figured hockey was a totally different world with totally different rules. You played hockey to win, got away with what you could, and let the referees decide what was right or wrong. You did what you had to do to be one of the guys in the locker room. So why should Franky think sports had anything to do with what I believed as a Christian?

▼ ▼ ▼ ▼ ▼

The next night we beat the WinterHawks 5-0 in front of a big home crowd. A bunch of kids waited for us in the lobby of the ice arena after the game.

"Guys!" one of the kids shouted as we stepped into sight. "There's Joey Hassrock!"

Ten of them crowded around me. This was fun, signing hockey programs. It made me feel like a real hero.

A freckle-faced little redhead kid pushed a program at me.

"How ya doing, bud? What's your name?"

"You don't know?" he asked. "We go to the same church. I always wave at you after, when church gets out."

"Yeah, that's right," I said. I thought quickly. "I just don't know how to *spell* your name."

He bought my little lie and smiled at me. Just another Hassrock Classic. Small, but classic.

"J-E-F-F," he told me. "Not G-E-O-F-F."

I signed.

"You're the coolest," he said. "Even if Dad says you're a dirty hockey player and cheat like crazy. But Dad's not really with it when it comes to sports. He doesn't understand you're supposed to do everything you can to win hockey games."

Somehow I managed to keep grinning. But it felt like the kid had whacked me between the eyes with a hockey stick. If my conscience was trying to tell me something, it was sure getting a lot of help.

▼ ▼ ▼ ▼ ▼

Next we played the Rebels. A win would keep us in first place. We wanted it bad.

With three minutes left in the game, it was 4-4. I skated onto the ice for a face-off in our end of the ice. The roar of the crowd was so loud I had to stand real close to one of our defensemen, John Oxford, to speak to him.

"If you get the puck," I said. "Fire it around behind the net. I'll be racing up along the boards. We might catch them by surprise."

It became one of those few times that a plan actually works. When the ref dropped the puck, our center managed to slap the puck to Oxford back at the defense position.

Instead of making the expected safe pass to our other defenseman, Oxford spun around and slammed the puck behind the net so that it followed the curve of the boards around the ice. It caught their defenseman by surprise and bounced past him to where I was already sprinting up the ice at full speed. I scooped the puck with my stick and raced toward their goalie—no one between us! A breakaway!

I busted up the ice as hard as I could. Their defenseman was doing the same as he chased me. *Ten more steps and I could shoot! Five more! Two more!*

Their defenseman reached out with his hockey stick and hooked my midsection. I started to fall. But this was no

Hassrock Classic—I was not faking this fall to draw a tripping penalty.

I tumbled onto my face, my arms and stick in front of me, sliding toward the goalie flat on my stomach. The puck dribbled ahead of me. I pushed at it with my stick and hands. The puck bounced off my hockey glove and slipped between the goalie's legs into the net. *I'd scored!*

Seconds later, my teammates reached me, lifting me to my feet and pounding my back.

I looked over their shoulders at the referee, to see if he had noticed how I'd scored. If he had seen me shovel the puck with my hand, the goal would be disallowed.

He wasn't waving off the goal. It would count. He thought I'd used my stick. We'd win on a Hassrock Classic . . . if I kept my mouth shut.

I didn't dare look in the stands. I knew Jeff would be watching this game, and I was afraid I'd see his face to remind me of the question I wanted to ignore. If it was okay to be a Christian in church but a cheat in hockey, why did I feel so terrible about the way the kid looked up to me?

Hardly knowing I was doing it, I skated over to the referee.

"Sir," I said, raising my voice above the roar of the crowd, "I pushed the puck into the net with my hand. It shouldn't be a goal."

There. I'd said it. I'd taken my beliefs and put them into action on the ice. The guys and coach would kill me for throwing the game away. But instead of feeling bad, I felt like a weight had been taken off my shoulders.

The referee was smiling at me. "That's a tough call to make on yourself, kid. You should be proud of yourself."

He blew the whistle and waved his arms, disallowing

the goal. My teammates stared at me in disbelief. I tried to keep my chin level as I skated toward the player's bench.

"Hassrock," the referee shouted. "Where are you going?"

I turned back. "Sir?"

"Hey, the guy tripped you on a breakaway. I was going to call the penalty until the puck went in the net. The goal might not count, but the penalty now does. And you know what that means, don't you?"

I did know.

Get tripped on a breakaway, you get a penalty shot. Just you and the goalie, with everyone watching from the side of the rink. You wait with the puck at center ice, and when the ref blows his whistle, you start the breakaway over again— a call so rare it only happens once or twice a season.

Did I score on the penalty shot?

Not even a problem. I was so excited to get a second chance, I ripped a shot the goalie would have had trouble seeing on a slow-motion replay.

And yes, we won on that goal. The papers made a big deal that I'd had the honesty to make a call against myself. It felt good, reading the newspaper, but not as good as having Jeff's dad shake my hand after church as he thanked me for showing his son a different way to play hockey.

Of course, the guys called it another Hassrock Classic. I let them, knowing soon enough they'd realize I was finished with the old classics.

WHAT'S UP THIS WEEK?

- Integrity
- More than a Sunday Christian
- Old Nature vs. New Nature

PRAYER POWER

Lots to talk about this week! Have you ever caught yourself doing your own version of a Hassrock Classic? We all have tried to get away with more than we should, not showing much integrity at times. Talk to God about it; ask him to show you what he has for you to learn this week.

INTEGRITY

Okay, so we've got the week's theme of being a consistent Christian. Today's topic is integrity, which means consistently dealing with others honestly and doing what's right even when it's difficult. Let's discover how integrity plays a part in living out a daily faith in Christ.

BRAIN STRETCHERS
FOR KIDS:

1. What is a Hassrock Classic? What are two examples from the story?
2. What do you think of the way Joey played hockey at the beginning of the story?
3. What does it mean to be consistent?

ASK AN ADULT:

1. Can you remember a time when you felt good about choosing to be a person of integrity?
2. Do you ever act a certain way because you know your actions will influence the whole family, like Joey's actions influenced Jeff?

SCRIPTURE POWER

The Lord has already told you what is good, and this is what he requires: to do what is right, to love mercy, and to walk humbly with your God. (Micah 6:8)

All he does is just and good, and all his commandments are trustworthy. They are forever true, to be obeyed faithfully and with integrity. (Psalm 111:7-8)

God has given us a blueprint for life, set out in the Bible. The Bible is a collection of true stories, historical events, and recorded words of Jesus—all of which are designed to help us live life the way God wants us to. We are to do what is right.

The Lord hates people with twisted hearts, but he delights in those who have integrity. (Proverbs 11:20)

These were his instructions to them: "You must always act in the fear of the Lord, with integrity and with undivided hearts." (2 Chronicles 19:9)

Joey's heart was divided. He wasn't acting with integrity when he tried to see how much he could get away with. His number one goal was to win at all costs—until he was faced with how inconsistent his character was. Integrity isn't real unless it affects our whole life.

Declare me innocent, O Lord, for I have acted with integrity; I have trusted in the Lord without wavering. Put me on trial, Lord, and cross-examine me. Test my motives and affections. (Psalm 26:1-2)

A person who lives with integrity and does what is right can pray the above verse free of guilt, because he knows God sees everything. Even our motives.

Happy are people of integrity, who follow the law of the Lord. (Psalm 119:1)

PRAYER POWER

What situations cause your integrity to waver? Do you want to be a person of integrity—someone people can count on to do the right thing? If so, then commit to praying about it regularly, beginning now. If you ask God to grow you in this area, he definitely will.

MORE THAN A SUNDAY CHRISTIAN

Yesterday we talked about integrity and how it needs to affect each area of our life—consistently. Let's talk more about that consistency so we make sure we're not just being "Sunday Christians."

BRAIN STRETCHERS
FOR KIDS:
1. Is it sometimes difficult for you to act like a Christian? at school? around certain people? in certain situations?
2. We're all imperfect, and we all mess up at times. How do you feel when you realize you haven't acted like a Christian?

ASK AN ADULT:
1. Same question for you: Is it sometimes difficult for you to act like a Christian? at work? around certain people? in certain situations?
2. Why wouldn't it be good for you to be just a "Sunday Christian"?

SCRIPTURE POWER

So get rid of all the filth and evil in your lives, and humbly accept the message God has planted in your hearts, for it is strong enough to save your souls. And remember, it is a message to obey, not just to listen to. If you don't obey, you are only fooling yourself. For if you just listen and don't obey, it is like looking at your face in a mirror but doing nothing to improve your appearance. You see yourself, walk away, and forget what you look like. But if you keep looking steadily into God's perfect law—the law that sets you free—and if you do what it says and don't forget what you heard, then God will bless you for doing it. (James 1:21-25)

Joey went to church and did the good Christian thing on Sundays, but his actions throughout the week didn't hold up. He was demonstrating what the above verses say about looking in a mirror and forgetting what you look like. He was a fair-weather friend to God, obeying him only when conditions were just right. Take a look at what God thinks of that:

I know all the things you do, that you are neither hot nor cold. I wish you were one or the other! But since you are like lukewarm water, I will spit you out of my mouth! (Revelation 3:15-16)

Think you can see how much you can get away with in life? Sometimes it seems simpler to separate our church life from the rest of what we do. Christianity doesn't work that way, though; you really can't be a sincere believer and just be a "Sunday Christian." When we submit our life to God, we are making a commitment to obey him on a daily basis. It's important to God that our behavior stay consistent in every area of life.

Be very careful to obey all the commands and the law that Moses gave to you. Love the Lord your God, walk in all his ways, obey his commands, be faithful to him, and serve him with all your heart and all your soul. (Joshua 22:5)

All. That's a big word in a small package—only three letters, but it packs a punch. *All.* Every bit—thoughts, actions, and words. God asks for our all, and that means every day of our lives and every part of each day.

So be strong! Be very careful to follow all the instructions written in the Book of the Law of Moses. Do not deviate from them in any way. (Joshua 23:6)

Well done, my good and faithful servant. You have been faithful in handling this small amount, so now I will give you many more responsibilities. Let's celebrate together! (Matthew 25:21)

The above two verses are a charge and a reward. The first one is a command to remain strong and obedient to God's ways. It takes endurance to go the distance, to stick it out and be successful in anything. But just imagine hearing God speak the words of the second verse to you: "Well done, my good and faithful servant. . . . Let's celebrate together!" What a party!

PRAYER POWER

Do you want to be more than a Sunday Christian? Do you want people to see a strong, consistently godly character in you? God wants to work on that with everyone. Find out what he has to say to you. Pray about it. He'll show you for sure.

OLD NATURE VS. NEW NATURE

In our quest to become consistent Christians, we've discussed integrity and being more than Sunday Christians. Now it's time to look more deeply into another aspect. This one's at the crux of our struggle—the central issue at the core of who we are and why we battle so much with sin. It's the problem of our old sin nature.

BRAIN STRETCHERS

FOR KIDS:

1. What did Joey think would happen when he told the truth about using his hand to score the goal at the end? Can you relate to his struggle to do the right thing?

2. Do you understand what your old sin nature is (before you became a Christian) and what your new nature in Christ is? If yes, then explain. If no, then today's reading will help you understand it.

ASK AN ADULT:

1. Do adults ever have a hard time getting rid of their old nature?

2. What do you do when you need help to live in your new nature?

SCRIPTURE POWER

[God] sent his own Son in a human body like ours, except that ours are sinful. God destroyed sin's control over us by giving his Son as a sacrifice for our sins. For the sinful nature is always hostile to God. It never did obey God's laws, and it never will. That's why those who are still under the control of their sinful nature can never please God. But you are not controlled by your sinful nature. You are controlled by the Spirit if you have the Spirit of God living in you. (And remember that those who do not have the Spirit of Christ living in them are not Christians at all.) (Romans 8:3, 7-9)

When we accept Jesus as Savior, he replaces our old nature with a new one. But old habits die hard, and it takes time and effort to consistently live in Jesus' strength when our old nature keeps tempting us with old ways.

And so, dear brothers and sisters, I plead with you to give your bodies to God. Let them be a living and holy sacrifice—the kind he will accept. When you think of what he has done for you, is this too much to ask? Don't copy the behavior and customs of this world, but let God transform you into a new person by changing the way you think. Then you will know what God wants you to do, and you will know how good and pleasing and perfect his will really is. (Romans 12:1-2)

Everybody wants to win, and most people are willing to

practice diligently and play hard to make it happen. Sometimes we get so selfish, though, that we are tempted to do something unfairly in order to win. Our sinful nature pushes us to do whatever it takes to make sure that we come out on top. When we surrender our life to God, we are making a commitment to saying no to our sinful nature and giving God control of our life. Cheating and dishonesty will not go unpunished. People who get rich by taking advantage of others will get the punishment they deserve. We may be tempted to follow in the footsteps of people who are dishonest, because they seem to be enjoying their lifestyle. However, we must remember that God will judge them, just as he will judge us. We need to surrender our life in obedience to God.

PRAYER POWER

We're nearly at the end of the week. What areas of your old nature do you need to give to God and let him change? Spending time reading God's Word and praying are key elements to making it in the Christian life. Pray that God will keep working on you, helping you win out over your old nature on a daily basis.

CONCLUDING THOUGHTS

In "A Hassrock Classic," Joey Hassrock tried to separate his hockey life from his Christianity. He justified his dishonesty on the ice by focusing on winning at all costs. He bent the rules as far as he could without getting caught, in order to help the team get a win. The referees were there to make the call, and if he could get away with a little cheating and they didn't see it, that was all part of the game, right?

Joey knew he couldn't continue to be just a "Sunday Christian." A little red-headed kid in his church challenged Joey to change his ways—even though the kid didn't know it! Joey decided to change his approach in hockey and in life. Their team won't win every game, but he sure will be able to sleep better at night!

As a result of his choice to show integrity, Joey's example of how to be more than a Sunday Christian had a good influence on Jeff. And Joey's old sin nature was beaten down a little more.

How can you work on becoming a more consistent Christian?

LINE IT UP!

Do you know what accountability is? It involves admitting to each other our weaknesses and struggles with sin and encouraging each other toward more obedience in following God's ways. When friends really care about helping each other grow strong, they will want to keep each other accountable, and they'll learn to welcome accountability in return. It's awesome that God knows we need each other's help to live the Christian life.

So . . . find an accountability partner. It should be someone who knows your junk—the mistakes and sins that trip you up. Take it seriously! You can really help each other.

If there's no one in your life now who would be a strong accountability partner, pray about it. God will be faithful to bring the right friend into your life in his perfect time. Maybe that person is right in your own family.

PRAYER POWER

Close the week with a few moments of quietness before God. You don't need to say anything to him right away. Just ask him to clear your mind of everything else so you can hear his voice more clearly. Listen closely. He will speak to your heart when you're willing to hear. God bless!

WEEK 6

WHAT'S UP THIS WEEK:
A True Leader

THEME VERSES FOR THE WEEK:
Hebrews 2:9-10

By God's grace, Jesus tasted death for everyone in all the world. And it was only right that God—who made everything and for whom everything was made—should bring his many children into glory. Through the suffering of Jesus, God made him a perfect leader.

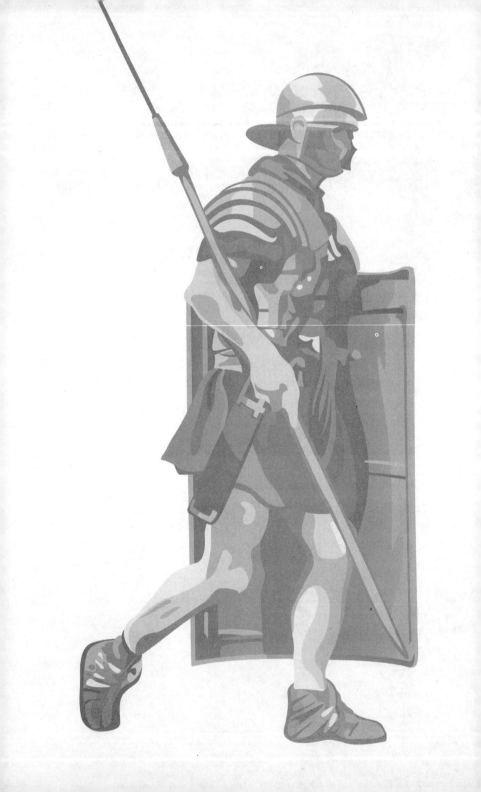

We all have had life-changing experiences at some point. In this story, Marcus encounters one beyond imagining. He witnesses true leadership happening as he watches his Savior being betrayed into the hands of killers. How will his life be altered?

Editor's Note: This historical fiction is based on the Scripture found in Matthew 26:47-56; Mark 14:43-52; Luke 22:47-53; and John 18:1-11. Portions of this may be found in Sigmund Brouwer's books *The Weeping Chamber* and *Into His Arms—Seeing Jesus through the Eyes of Children.*

In the Garden

Marcus was not yet asleep when the violent pounding on the outside door broke the silence of the darkened household. In his chamber, he sat upright on his sleeping mat, pulling his linen nightshirt tight around himself.

Bang! Bang! Bang!

Loud, angry shouts came with the pounding.

"We demand entry by authority of the governor of Judea!"

Soldiers? Roman soldiers? Marcus hugged himself. In Jerusalem, even during daylight, everyone feared the soldiers. Now they were here at night! But why?

Moments later, Marcus heard his father at the door. It took some time for his father to lift the wooden bar that held the door secure. Through the arched doorway of his chamber, Marcus saw the flickering light of oil lamps. Soldiers' footsteps echoed through the house. Then they neared his chamber.

From his place on the bed, Marcus squinted against lamplight as soldiers entered and briefly searched his room.

"Where is he? The man named Jesus," one demanded of Marcus. All Marcus saw were the dark shadows of the large soldiers behind the light. "I . . . I . . . don't know," Marcus said.

"You saw him earlier tonight?"

Dazed by surprise, Marcus did not know how to answer. Yes, he'd seen the rabbi Jesus, for Marcus had helped prepare the upper room of his father's house for the rabbi's Passover celebration this Thursday night. Jesus had left barely a half hour earlier, taking his friends with him.

But these were Roman soldiers, armed with swords and spears. And Marcus knew that a bounty had been placed on the rabbi's head. What would happen to Jesus if he told the soldiers that Jesus had indeed been here? And what would happen, Marcus wondered, to his father for allowing Jesus in the house?

Marcus was saved the need to reply. Another man pushed into the light beside the soldier.

"I told you," this man said. He was a slim man, with a dark, neatly trimmed beard. His face had the handsomeness of a fox. "Jesus was here. I left this very house only a half hour ago."

Judas? One of the friends of Jesus? Marcus knew this man, for Marcus had greeted all of the men as they entered the house just after sunset.

But why, Marcus asked himself, *has Judas led soldiers and religious leaders back to the house? Why isn't Judas with the rabbi?*

With a grunt, the soldier turned away with his oil lamp.

As soon as he was alone in his chamber once again, Marcus stood from his sleeping mat. He moved to the doorway to listen to the conversation beyond.

Enough light showed that Marcus recognized chief priests among the soldiers. And Marcus saw another man he remembered from temple services.

Caiaphas! The high priest! He was tall and thin, with a hooked nose and the fearsome face that all Jews recognized. No other man in Jerusalem or all of Israel held more power!

Caiaphas stepped close to Judas.

"You make all of us look like fools," Caiaphas snarled. "Where is he?"

The torchlight threw dancing shadows across Judas as he screwed his eyes shut to think.

"There is only one place he would be at this hour," Judas said. "In a garden. It is called Gethsemane."

▼ ▼ ▼ ▼ ▼

Marcus was in such a hurry to follow that he did not waste any time throwing on outer garments or a cloak. He slipped into his sandals, sneaking out of the house and making his way onto the city streets as his father spoke in the courtyard with some of the soldiers.

105

Jesus! What would happen to Jesus? Marcus had to know.

He followed as the soldiers marched through the city and into the countryside. Some of the soldiers carried torches set on high poles, casting light around them to aid their search.

Marcus stayed with them. He was protected by the black of night, able to stay fairly close—close enough to hear conversations among the soldiers. Close enough to hear Caiaphas when the Roman captain stopped him.

"This man you seek," the captain said to the high priest. "How will we know him?"

It was Judas who answered, before Caiaphas could reply.

"There will be no mistake," Judas said. "I will greet him with a kiss."

▼ ▼ ▼ ▼ ▼

None of the soldiers appeared to notice Marcus as he slipped into the grove of olive trees. Marcus knew the place well. It was at the foot of the hill opposite the valley outside the walls of Jerusalem. From that spot, Marcus could see Jesus.

The shadows of the olive trees moved as the soldiers pushed forward with their torches. The outlines of the gnarled low branches seemed like ghosts trying to clutch at Marcus while he watched as the soldiers found Jesus.

But Marcus knew he was free to leave. This Jesus, the man of miracles, what was to happen to him? Marcus had to know. Perhaps he could even call out a warning.

From his spot safe in the deep shadows, Marcus saw Judas step forward from the mob of soldiers. Marcus watched Judas stretch out his arms toward Jesus. The other 11 men were huddled in a group behind Jesus, terrified by the sudden appearance of the Roman soldiers.

"Teacher!" Judas said.

No! Marcus wanted to cry out. *He betrays you!* But his fear of the soldiers was too great. So Marcus stayed in the shadows, watching with horror as Judas kissed Jesus on the cheek.

Jesus stepped around Judas. Marcus heard calmness in the rabbi's voice.

"Who is it you want?" Jesus asked.

The sound of that voice put a picture in Marcus's mind—a picture of a man with peace in his eyes, a picture of a man with a gentle touch. The man who had greeted Marcus earlier in the evening had looked Marcus in the eyes with a gaze that had seemed to touch Marcus's soul.

"Jesus of Nazareth." The replying soldier spoke like a bully facing a child.

"I am he," Jesus said.

His calm assurance sent hope into Marcus's heart. After all, this was the man whom people said had walked across water. Why should Jesus fear soldiers?

Marcus saw immediately that some of the soldiers had the same thoughts. This was not a man frightened by the full authority of the Roman empire. No, this was one who acted as if he, not they, controlled the situation. A man, then, who actually might have performed the miracles the tales of which had reached the soldiers' ears in the fortress above the temple.

Their quick reaction was the result of a superstitious fear of some divine punishment. The soldiers closest to Jesus stepped back and stumbled to the feet of the soldiers directly behind them, who then tripped and fell to the ground.

Marcus nearly giggled, for swords and shields clanked as soldiers scrambled to their feet. The rest of the mob had begun to press in, and there was no place for the soldiers to flee.

"Who is it you want?" Jesus asked again.

"Jesus of Nazareth." This time, the soldier's answer was respectful.

"I told you that I am he," Jesus said. He swung his right arm to point at the disciples huddled behind him. "If you are looking for me, then let these men go."

Behind the soldiers, the centurion finally barked out orders, as if Jesus' reminder of the other 11 men snapped the centurion from his fear. For if the 11 men rushed the soldiers, fighting would be difficult in the crowd. A Roman sword could easily strike one of the chief priests—or worse, Caiaphas—and the political disaster from that would end the centurion's career.

"Now!" the centurion said. Once they were holding Jesus, the others would not dare attack. "Seize him!"

In the milling confusion of figures and shadows beneath flickering torchlight, Marcus saw the fisherman named Peter move around the edge of the mob. He saw Peter withdraw a short sword hidden beneath his cloak.

It would have been crazy to attack one of the armed soldiers. It would have been equally crazy to injure a chief priest or the high priest himself, so Peter moved toward one of the servants instead.

Peter did not want his defense to go unnoticed by Jesus. Judas had betrayed Jesus. Peter would do the opposite.

"Lord!" Peter shouted as he swung. "Should we strike them with our swords?"

The servant jumped sideways at Peter's warning cry, and the sword sliced along his skull, shearing off part of his ear.

"No more of this!" Jesus commanded. Although a soldier was about to grab him, Jesus stepped away unhindered. No one made a move to stop him as he reached the whimpering servant.

Jesus put his left arm around the servant's slight shoulders to comfort him. With his right hand, Jesus touched the man's ear; and when Jesus pulled his hand away to examine it in the torchlight, Marcus saw blood.

"Put your sword back in its place," he said to Peter, "for all who draw the sword will die by the sword."

Marcus saw and heard all of it clearly. He was frozen in place, drawn by all of the action.

"Do you not know I could call on my Father," Jesus said to Peter, "and he would at once put at my disposal thousands of angels?"

Perhaps Jesus realized that Peter still needed instruction, as do all children of God. Jesus' voice softened. "But how then would the Scriptures be fulfilled that say it must happen in this way?"

As calmly as he had stepped away from the arresting soldiers, Jesus returned to them. Because all attention was on him, none immediately noticed the servant he had left behind, who was now touching his ear in great wonder, amazed that the bleeding and pain had ended.

None, perhaps, except Marcus, who would remember this night as long as he lived.

The appearance of resistance had been enough for the centurion. He commanded the soldiers nearest him to arrest Jesus immediately.

Other soldiers moved to capture the disciples, but they fled into the shadows of the trees, passing by Marcus's hiding place.

Then a pursuing soldier saw Marcus!

Marcus was caught by surprise. The soldier's strong hands grabbed Marcus, who twisted in panic. Marcus spun away only by slipping from his linen garment. The soldier began to chase.

"We have who we need!" yelled the centurion. The last thing he wanted was his soldiers running around in the darkness beyond the torchlight. "Return and regroup!"

The crashing through the small brush of the olive grove behind Marcus ended. He was safe. He didn't keep running. He had seen too much to leave now. He knew he must see the end of this.

Marcus crept back. Safe again in the shadows, with all the attention on the rabbi Jesus, Marcus watched as soldiers tightened a rope around Jesus' wrists.

Jesus looked over the heads of the soldiers at the chief priests and their servants.

Marcus heard Jesus challenge them, unafraid.

"Am I leading a rebellion, so that you have come with swords and clubs? Every day I was with you in the temple courts, and you did not lay a hand on me."

With all his command around him, the centurion began to lead captive Jesus back to Jerusalem. Jesus would be silent for the entire journey, but he had some last words for the chief priests.

"This is your hour," he said, "when darkness reigns."

▼ ▼ ▼ ▼ ▼

The darkness for Jesus continued through an illegal trial. It continued through death as a result of the public torture of crucifixion.

All of this darkness filled Marcus with great grief.

But the darkness reigned only three days.

On Sunday, late in the morning, Marcus heard the news: The tomb of Jesus had been found empty! And this despite the fact that it had been guarded by Roman soldiers—soldiers who faced death if they failed in their duty. Despite the fact that the stone in front of the tomb was so heavy that one man alone could not move it.

The tomb was empty.

Peter himself was spreading the word.

Jesus was alive!

Editor's note: For Marcus, this may have been the most important night of his life—a night of destiny. Because of these events, he became a follower of Jesus, a helper of the apostle Paul, mentioned by name in Paul's letters in the New Testament. But that is not all. Many historians believe it was this boy who later gathered the complete story of Jesus from years of listening to the disciple Peter. If so, there was one scene added as a result of this boy's own unique witness: the scene in the garden when the soldier grabs him and his garment. And this scene forever endures in the Gospel named after this boy: The Gospel according to Mark.

WHAT'S UP THIS WEEK?

- Peaceful Strength
- Powerful Wisdom
- Selfless Servanthood

PRAYER POWER

Being a leader takes training and a sincere heart. Now is the time, when you're young, to ask God to prepare you and help you to be a leader someday. Expect him to show you what it means to be a true leader worthy of respect.

PEACEFUL STRENGTH

Every once in a while something happens to radically change your life. Marcus was changed forever by the events that took place in the Garden of Gethsemane. He witnessed Jesus' actions as a leader, and Marcus grew in leadership, sharing boldly the message of Jesus Christ. Let's look at what this defining moment watching Jesus taught Marcus about peaceful strength.

BRAIN STRETCHERS

FOR KIDS:

1. What thoughts or feelings did you have while reading the story? Did you want Jesus to fight back when the soldiers arrested him? Why do you think he didn't?
2. What do you think it would have been like to be in Marcus's place that night? Would you have responded differently than he did?
3. What do you think of Judas?

ASK AN ADULT:

1. Is there really such a thing as peaceful strength?

2. How was Jesus showing peaceful strength when he didn't fight the soldiers?
3. Was there ever a time for you when responding calmly would have made a situation better?

SCRIPTURE POWER

He was led as a sheep to the slaughter. And as a lamb is silent before the shearers, he did not open his mouth. (Acts 8:32)

Maybe you're still asking yourself just what peaceful strength is. The verse above puts more definition to it. Think for a minute about who Jesus was. He was the *Son of God.* He had the guts to die a gruesome death on the cross, after being mocked and beaten for hours. Jesus was no wimp. With calm strength, he walked into the most torturous event of all time. But how does this show true leadership? Check out the next verse.

Peace and righteousness will be your leaders! Violence will disappear from your land. . . . Salvation will surround you like city walls, and praise will be on the lips of all who enter there. (Isaiah 60:17-18)

See there? Peace and righteousness—leadership qualities that are more powerful than violence and lead others to praise God.

In quietness and confidence is your strength. (Isaiah 30:15)

Godly character is the most important element of being a leader. Studying God's Word will help you get to know him

113

better and become more like him. He'll develop in you the peaceful strength you'll need for whatever leadership roles he has in store for you.

PRAYER POWER

Do you need to develop more of Jesus' type of peaceful strength? There's no room for hotheads in leadership. Pray about it now, and ask God for more awareness of how you respond to stressful situations. He'll help you grow in calm strength.

POWERFUL WISDOM

What's next in our quest to be true leaders? Well, leaders who are truly godly need lots of wisdom. Wisdom means more than just knowing a lot or being the smartest. It involves responsibility, common sense, sensitivity, and a commitment to doing the right thing even when it's difficult. A wise person has the big picture in mind and is willing to pay the price of obedience. Let's find out more about wisdom.

BRAIN STRETCHERS
FOR KIDS:

1. Why is it important for leaders to be wise?
2. Do you know kids in school whom others kids follow? Do you think the qualities that make those people leaders are the right qualities? What qualities are those?
3. Would you follow yourself as a leader? Why or why not? Do you stand up for the right values?

ASK AN ADULT:

1. Is there a difference between knowing a lot and being wise?

2. Who are some of the leaders you follow, and why?
3. Have you ever been a leader—in school, at church, at work? How did you become a good leader?

SCRIPTURE POWER

If God has given you leadership ability, take the responsibility seriously. (Romans 12:8)

You should take a leadership role seriously because you're in a position to influence others. Leaders are watched by others, and they set the example to follow.

A wise person is stronger than the ten leading citizens of a town! (Ecclesiastes 7:19)

The verse above tells us that there are leaders who are not necessarily the wisest people. Can you think of any leaders like that? One of today's Brain Stretchers asked if there are kids in school who may or may not have the best character qualities, but other kids still may follow them. This verse says that there's more strength in being wise. Wise people make better leaders.

I will give you leaders after my own heart, who will guide you with knowledge and understanding. (Jeremiah 3:15)

Good leaders are ones who follow God. That's what this verse means by "after my own heart." A wise leader will guide people with understanding and will follow God's example. In other words, that leader will show compassion, kindness, and other godly characteristics to others.

116

Without wise leadership, a nation falls. (Proverbs 11:14)

That's your final verse for the day. The impact of good and bad leadership can be huge! Entire nations can and have fallen because of bad leadership. Is your leadership the kind that builds people up or tears them down?

PRAYER POWER

Talk to God today about wisdom. Ask him to help you understand it more. When a person is committed to doing things God's way, God is more than happy to provide that person with all the wisdom he or she needs to accomplish the task.

SELFLESS SERVANTHOOD

There are many qualities that make a good leader. The list could be endless. We're going to talk about one more specific quality this week—one that happens to be a biggie. It's the quality of being a selfless servant.

BRAIN STRETCHERS
FOR KIDS:

1. What does it mean to be a servant? Would you rather be a servant or be someone in charge? Why?
2. Did Jesus act like a servant or like the boss?

ASK AN ADULT:

1. Can you think of some leaders who remind you of Jesus because they are willing to serve other people?
2. How do you feel when a leader just wants to give orders instead of being willing to help people?

SCRIPTURE POWER

Jesus called them together and said, "You know that in this world kings are tyrants, and officials lord it over the people beneath them. But among you it should be quite different. Whoever wants to be a leader among you must be your servant, and whoever wants to be first must become your slave. For even I, the Son of Man, came here not to be served but to serve others, and to give my life as a ransom for many." (Matthew 20:25-28)

Jesus taught that a good leader is someone who serves the people he leads. That may or may not sound like a good plan to you, but Jesus backed it up with action. He did the absolute most servantlike thing by dying for guilty sinners. He was perfect, yet he gave his life for us, a whole lot of imperfect people.

But among you, those who are the greatest should take the lowest rank, and the leader should be like a servant. Normally the master sits at the table and is served by his servants. But not here! For I am your servant. You have remained true to me in my time of trial. And just as my Father has granted me a Kingdom, I now grant you the right to eat and drink at my table in that Kingdom. And you will sit on thrones, judging the twelve tribes of Israel. (Luke 22:26-30)

A leader who serves unselfishly has other people's best interests in mind. He doesn't want to rule over everyone. Instead, he wants to see other people grow. Notice this phrase toward the end of those verses: "You will sit on thrones." A servant leader doesn't want to hold others back so he can keep bossing them around. Quite the opposite. He wants to see others advance to positions of honor.

PRAYER POWER

Selfless servanthood may be the toughest part of leadership. Without a doubt we all can be selfish at times. None of us feels like giving to others all the time. We need God's help to become better at this. So talk to God about this; ask him to help you be a better servant. God will honor that desire in you, and other people will grow to respect you for it.

CONCLUDING THOUGHTS

Defining moments are those events that happen that truly make a difference in our life. As we live from moment to moment and day to day, we are constantly learning and being changed. But every once in a while, something really big happens—something that grows our potential to make a difference in the lives of others, something that prepares us for leadership.

Most good leaders could probably tell you about events that impacted their lives and led to their positions of influence. Godly leaders will tell you that it is impossible to do your best without depending on God for wisdom. Encounters with our Savior make the most powerful defining moments.

In the story "In the Garden," Marcus had already been moved by Jesus. He was so caught up in the events surrounding Jesus that he couldn't help but follow the soldiers out to the Garden of Gethsemane. The events that happened while he was there formed a defining moment for Marcus. Because of what transpired there, his life would never be the same. God was preparing him for leadership.

God allows things to happen in our life for a reason. The Bible says that he works everything together for good, when we are called for his purpose. He wants us to have defining moments, which change our life forever, so that our life from that moment on is lived in closer friendship with him. Then we will have what it takes to be godly leaders.

How has knowing Jesus changed you? Do you want him to prepare you to be a leader?

LINE IT UP!

This week's "Line It Up!" involves writing a personal mission statement. *Huh?* Okay, here's the deal:

We all need goals in life. Having a goal brings perspective and helps us know who we are and what we're about. A mission statement is a written way to define that.

It can be whatever length you need it to be to say what you want it to say. Keep in mind, though, that it will be easier to remember if it's relatively short. Take some time with it. Think about what you really want other people to see in you. What matters most? Do you want them to see God's love first of all? maybe his joy or strength? maybe his servant leadership?

Here's a good example of a short mission statement: "I want Jesus' power and love to grow in me so others will see it and want to know him better."

When you figure out what you want your mission statement to be, write it down and keep it somewhere visible where you'll see it every day.

PRAYER POWER

We're done with another week! What have you learned?
Maybe you're feeling a little scared about being a leader.
It can be a tough responsibility. Keep in mind that a good
leader knows how to follow others, too. Ask God to keep
speaking to you about leadership. He'll show you specifically
what he has in mind for you to do. God bless!

WEEK 7

WHAT'S UP THIS WEEK:
True Success

THEME VERSES FOR THE WEEK:
Philippians 3:8-9

Yes, everything else is worthless when compared with the priceless gain of knowing Christ Jesus my Lord. I have discarded everything else, counting it all as garbage, so that I may have Christ and become one with him. I no longer count on my own goodness or my ability to obey God's law, but I trust Christ to save me.

Frank and Joe Hardly are used to doing things well. In fact, their accomplishments are so impressive that it seems they never do anything wrong! In this week's story, however, they're faced with an intriguing mystery that has them stumped. Can they figure out the clues before it's too late to save their lives?

The Hardly Boys

"Frank! Joe!" Chet Mountain exclaimed. His voice echoed through the large Hardly Boys house and reached Frank and Joe where they were exercising in their basement gym. "Come to the front door! On the double!"

"Wow," said the handsome, blond 17-year-old Joe Hardly as he sprang to his feet from where he was finishing a set of 200 sit-ups. "Chet sounds like he's worried. Maybe it's another mystery!"

Frank, who was dark-haired, equally handsome, and a year older than his brother, mopped sweat from his forehead. "It's a good thing I'm done with my 200 push-ups," Frank said. "As stars of the high school football team, we can't get lazy."

Joe grinned at his brother. Then they sprinted up the stairs, three steps at a time.

Chet Mountain was waiting for them at the open front door. Their chubby pal often went along with the Hardly Boys to look for clues. He lived on a farm about a mile from their town of Booport.

"What's up?" Frank queried.

Chet pointed at the front lawn, his face white and his chubby finger quivering fearfully.

Patches of brown dead grass were visible on the lush green lawn. The dead grass formed huge words that reached from one side of the lawn to the other.

FRANK AND JOE, YOU WON'T LIVE FOREVER.

Joe snapped his fingers. "Frank, last night someone must have poured concentrated weed killer on the lawn . . . "

" . . . destroying the grass in the shape of the words," Frank Hardly finished. "Maybe one of the criminals we threw into jail has now been released and is out to get us."

"You're not afraid?" Chet asked.

Joe gave him a confident grin. "The Hardly Boys? We've solved over 100 mysteries."

"That's right," Frank chimed in, "and we're not even out of high school. Plus we can each do hundreds of sit-ups and push-ups and star in any sport we want. We're not afraid of anything."

"Not even your spinster aunt?" a voice interrupted from behind them.

"Aunt Grosstrude!" Frank and Joe said at the same time as they spun around.

Aunt Grosstrude was a tall, stern-looking woman with a twinkle in her eyes and a tray with cookies and milk in her hands. "With your famous detective mother and father gone

128

to trace a missing nuclear warhead, I have to make sure you have plenty to eat. Now what's the fuss?"

She set the tray down. Frank and Joe showed her the threat on the lawn.

"Oh, dear!" Aunt Grosstrude exclaimed. "This sounds serious."

"We'll get to the bottom of this," Joe vowed with a serious look.

"Come on, Joe," Frank urged. "Let's go to the police station right now and ask Chief Crowllig for a list of recently released criminals."

They sprinted to their car, a red roadster donated by a grateful jeweler who wanted to reward Frank and Joe for recovering a million-dollars-worth of diamonds. Chet Mountain stayed behind to keep eating cookies.

Ten minutes later, Frank and Joe were at the police station. Fifteen minutes later, they were back in their roadster.

"That's strange," Frank said puzzledly. "No recently released criminals."

"Remember," Joe pointed out, "Chief Crowllig said that's because we did such good work getting them behind bars."

Frank brightened. Then his face dimmed.

"Say, Joe," he asked seriously as they drove, "do you smell something funny?"

"Yes, Frank," Joe said. "Almost like someone has smeared Limburger cheese on our exhaust pipe, knowing that it would bake onto the heated metal and smell terrible for weeks."

Sure enough, when they pulled over, they discovered that was exactly what had happened. Unexpectedly, they also found a warning scratched into the baked, smelly cheese:
FRANK AND JOE, YOU WON'T LIVE FOREVER.

Frank and Joe looked at each other and grinned.

"Mysteries are such fun, aren't they?" Joe queried.

"Especially because we never let them interfere with getting top grades at school," Frank replied.

Over the next two weeks, however, Frank and Joe Hardly began to worry.

Every day the mysterious threatener found many ways to warn them.

Once, he put a garden hose in the mail slot of the front door. Then he rang the doorbell and turned on the water. It gushed into the balloon at the end of the hose. Without the doorbell warning, the balloon would have burst in the hallway, ruining the priceless heirloom rug given to Frank and Joe as a reward for saving Mexico from a dynamite-triggered earthquake. Instead, Frank and Joe pointed the hose outside, sprinted to the faucet, and turned the water off, only to find another note taped to the faucet. It read: *FRANK AND JOE, YOUR DAYS ON EARTH ARE NUMBERED.*

A few days later, the phone rang. Joe was writing a 200-page essay on the ideals of democracy for his high school history class, using the computer which was a reward for stopping all the secrets of the CIA from being leaked to Saddam Hussein. Joe sprinted to the telephone in the upstairs hallway.

"Hello," he said. "World-famous Hardly Boys residence."

Joe only heard a dial tone. As he hung up, puzzled, he noticed a note taped to the side of the phone.

"Frank!" Joe called. "Are you finished with your 200 push-ups?"

Frank sprinted up the stairs from the gym in the basement. Joe grimly apprised him of the situation.

"Another note," Frank said in a hushed voice as he opened it. "I'll bet it's another warning."

It was. *FRANK AND JOE, YOU WON'T LIVE FOREVER.*

"I'm getting worried," Joe said. "How did the intruder manage to intrude right into our house?"

"Worse," Frank said. "Your ear is black from where you pressed the telephone receiver against it."

"No," Joe groaned. "Did I fall for the old shoe-polish-on-the-telephone-receiver trick?"

"I'm afraid so," Frank replied. "Joe, face it. This mystery is baffling us."

The final straw for the sleuths came when Frank went into the dining room the next evening. He flicked the light switch, but darkness remained and he jumped back at a small popping sound. Immediately a horrible smell of sulfur and rotten eggs hit his face.

"Joe," he cried. "Something unusual!"

"Do I need the fingerprint kit?" Joe called back from where he was stuck on the first page of a 200-page science essay he was writing about the eating habits of spicklebacked toads.

"No! Grab a flashlight," Frank shouted to him.

Joe took one from his desk drawer and sprinted down the stairs. Frank and Joe used the flashlight to survey the dining room.

"Obviously someone ran a wire from the empty lightbulb socket to a small stink bomb," Frank said. "When I flicked the switch, it exploded."

"Doesn't look like there's any damage, but what if it had been a real bomb?" Joe queried. He paused. "And look! A note taped beside the light switch."

Frank groaned. "You read it," he said despairingly. "I can't bear the pressure any longer."

"I can't read it either," Joe said. "I'm afraid it will be the same threat we've been receiving for weeks."

They both began to shed manly tears.

"What's this?" Aunt Grosstrude said as she walked out from the kitchen.

"Oh, Aunt Grosstrude," Joe wailed, "we can't solve this mystery! And it is bothering us so much we haven't been the usual stars in sports. Frank can barely do 100 push-ups now. And I even . . . " Joe Hardly's voice trembled further. "I even fell to a B+ on my last school assignment."

Joe wailed more. "And our car still stinks from the Limburger cheese on the exhaust pipe!"

"Yes," Frank sobbed. "We have no clues. Somehow the intruder slips in and out whenever he wants. What if next time he decides to try something deadly instead of just leaving notes?"

"What do you mean?" Aunt Grosstrude said with her usual stern face.

"Read the note on the wall!" they exclaimed.

Aunt Grosstrude set down her fresh, succulent pumpkin pie. She read the note aloud: *"FRANK AND JOE, YOU WON'T LIVE FOREVER."*

"See," Frank sniffed. "With these notes appearing all the time, how can we remain super detectives?"

"And super athletes and super students?" Joe interjected mournfully. "We're too worried that we're going to die!"

"Of course you are," Aunt Grosstrude said firmly.

"What?" Frank and Joe chorused.

"You *are* going to die some day. Surely you didn't expect to live forever, did you?"

"Well . . . " Frank began.

"It's not something we usually consider," Joe added.

"Which is exactly why I've been planting those notes," Aunt Grosstrude said.

"You!" Frank and Joe chorused again.

"Who else could come and go without being suspected?" she answered.

"Why?" Frank said, wiping a tear from his cheek.

"Because I'm worried about you guys. People who are successful often enjoy the success so much they forget it's what comes *after* this world that is truly important. It's too easy for them to become focused on themselves and to get selfish for more success. Let me ask you guys, do you ever think beyond your own triumphs?"

Frank and Joe shook their heads sadly.

"See what I mean?" Aunt Grosstrude said. "You've forgotten that there are much more important things than *your* rewards, *your* good grades, *your* victorious games, and *your* solved mysteries. If you don't look beyond your own selfish little worlds, you're going blindfolded through *this* world. I wanted those notes to remind you to live with your eyes on the next world and to think of what lies ahead."

"Wow!" Joe said. "What a lesson!"

"Exactly," Frank chimed in.

Both of them hugged their aunt.

"I'll open the windows," Joe volunteered.

"I'll get a fan to help clear the air," Frank offered. "This is one mystery I'm glad we didn't solve."

WHAT'S UP THIS WEEK?

- Who Defines Success?
- Who Gets the Credit?
- Who Are You Living For?

PRAYER POWER

Success is a big deal to a lot of people. Whether our thing is sports, grades, music, theater, or any other activity, we all want to be good at the things we enjoy doing. Ask God to show you this week what success looks like through *his* eyes. His views are very different from what the world tells us is important. Pray for an open heart and mind to hear what he has to say to you.

WHO DEFINES SUCCESS?

We all need wake-up calls every now and then to make us realize what's important. Frank and Joe were good guys who helped others, did well in school, and seemed successful in life. In short, they had it all going on. Or did they? Let's see how their lives weren't measuring up to God's definition of success.

BRAIN STRETCHERS

FOR KIDS:

1. What were some of the things the Hardly Boys were good at?
2. What do you think success meant to them?
3. Why was Aunt Grosstrude worried about Frank and Joe? By leaving the notes, what was she trying to help them realize about their lives?

ASK AN ADULT:

1. What do you think is real success in God's eyes?
2. In what ways does God's definition of success affect your decisions?

SCRIPTURE POWER

Stop fooling yourselves. If you think you are wise by this world's standards, you will have to become a fool so you can become wise by God's standards. For the wisdom of this world is foolishness to God. As the Scriptures say, "God catches those who think they are wise in their own cleverness." (1 Corinthians 3:18-19)

Aunt Grosstrude sent the Hardly Boys several wake-up calls in the form of mysterious notes to help them understand some important truths about paying attention to God's plan first of all.

I observed that most people are motivated to success by their envy of their neighbors. But this, too, is meaningless, like chasing the wind. (Ecclesiastes 4:4)

Have you heard the term "keeping up with the Joneses"? Most often it has to do with financial success and making sure you seem to have as much as—or more than—everyone else around you. But it can apply to other areas of life as well, such as sports, school, and popularity. We tend to want to impress other people with just how great we can be. But the above verse shows clearly that this attitude is meaningless.

As long as the king sought the Lord, God gave him success. (2 Chronicles 26:5)

Now, my son, may the Lord be with you and give you success as you follow his instructions. (1 Chronicles 22:11)

136 These verses show where true success lies: in following the Lord's instructions—focusing on him, seeking him, making him number one in our life. True success comes as we obey God.

PRAYER POWER

How do you define success? Who is your number one focus? We're surrounded by the world's opinions about what true success is, and it's often difficult to keep in mind what God says about success. Ask him to remind you each day of this truth: Success comes from putting God first!

WHO GETS THE CREDIT?

So we've gotten the idea that God views success differently than the world sees it. Then how should we view our accomplishments? Of course God wants us to feel good about ourselves and the things we do well. It's just that he wants the credit he rightfully deserves for giving us our talents and abilities and for helping us succeed.

BRAIN STRETCHERS

FOR KIDS:

1. In "The Hardly Boys," Frank and Joe were focused on themselves rather than on God. What happens when you focus too much on yourself and the things you're busy doing?
2. What talents and abilities has God given you? Are you ever tempted to take the credit for your skills?

ASK AN ADULT:

1. What is something you do well that you feel proud of?
2. Has there ever been a time when you've taken too much credit for the good things in your life instead of giving God the credit? When was that? What happened?

SCRIPTURE POWER

It is not that we think we can do anything of lasting value by ourselves. Our only power and success come from God. (2 Corinthians 3:5)

Being skilled at something is great, and working hard to do our best is a good thing. The problem with being great at something is that we can easily forget who gives us our skills and abilities. We can be proud of our accomplishments and hard work, but it's important to give credit where credit is due. Christian athletes will often begin an interview by first giving praise to God as their Savior. The athletes are not denying that they accomplished something good in their sport, but they are acknowledging that God gives them the skills and abilities they have.

[God] has made an everlasting covenant with me. His agreement is eternal, final, sealed. He will constantly look after my safety and success. (2 Samuel 23:5)

God is the one looking after our life, just as this verse says. Our success is entirely dependent on God's love for us. Because of all he's given to us, we can be assured of being truly successful—*by his definition.* He is pleased when we give our all to him. We'll talk more about that tomorrow.

PRAYER POWER

Today's lesson focused on giving God the credit for our abilities and achievements. Make today's prayer time a time to thank God for those things. Let him know you appreciate them, and give him the credit he deserves for all the ways he's blessed you.

WHO ARE YOU LIVING FOR?

Wow, today's topic is a tough one! We've discussed the true definition of success, and we've learned some things about giving God credit for our abilities. Now it's time to "put our money where our mouth is." It's time to ask ourselves, *Who are we living for—ourselves or God?*

BRAIN STRETCHERS
FOR KIDS:

1. In "The Hardly Boys," what things or goals were Frank and Joe putting ahead of God?
2. What things are you tempted to put ahead of God?

ASK AN ADULT:

1. Is there something or someone you are tempted to put ahead of God?
2. What do you do when you face those temptations?

SCRIPTURE POWER

I live in eager expectation and hope that I will never do anything that causes me shame, but that I will always be bold for Christ, as I have been in the past, and that my life will always honor Christ, whether I live or I die. (Philippians 1:20)

Frank and Joe were sidetracked by all they had going on in their lives. We, too, can get so wrapped up in our activities that they become our entire life's focus. The apostle Paul's entire purpose in life was to serve Christ. He wanted to glorify God through everything he did in life, in order that other people would come to know God too. Paul committed his life to serving others and didn't take the glory for any successes he had; instead, he used all of his life to praise God.

Instead of worshiping the glorious, ever-living God, they worshiped idols made to look like mere people, or birds and animals and snakes. (Romans 1:23)

Some people still worship idols carved of wood or stone, but there are also many other ways to idolize people or things. Any time we place something else ahead of God, we are making that thing an idol. We are turning away from the Creator and focusing our praise on the things that he has created. People who do this may think they are wise, but God calls them fools.

Yet if I live, that means fruitful service for Christ. I really don't know which is better. I'm torn between two desires: Sometimes I want to live, and sometimes I long to go and be with Christ. That would be far better for me. (Philippians 1:22-23)

Let's go back to the apostle Paul for a minute. Paul was very willing to continue serving God on Earth, and he wanted to

141

see all people come to know Christ. He was also excited about going to heaven! He knew that being with God in heaven would be the best thing possible—better than anything good on Earth could ever be. Because of this, he really looked forward to the time when God would call him home to heaven. His vision for his life was bigger than just earning the best grades or being seen as successful by the people around him. This is the message Aunt Grosstrude wanted Frank and Joe to understand. They needed to put God first. We need to do the same.

PRAYER POWER

Lots to digest this week! It's been full of important info and truths to think about. As you pray, ask God to show you more about true success and about giving him the credit for all he's given to you. Then step out in faith and make him your main focus each day.

CONCLUDING THOUGHTS

In "The Hardly Boys," Frank and Joe were great athletes, top students, accomplished detectives, and perfect sons. They didn't seem to do anything wrong! They were completely wrapped up in perfection and were very proud of all their accomplishments. It really bothered them that they couldn't seem to solve the mystery of the notes, which kept warning them that they wouldn't live forever. They used all their wits and abilities to try and solve the mystery and eventually found out their aunt had been planting the warning notes.

She was concerned that they were completely wrapped up in their accomplishments and abilities and weren't seeing God's big picture and purpose for them. The boys learned to appreciate the lesson of the notes.

God often gives us notes of warning along life's path and uses people around us to provide wake-up calls. These wake-up calls remind us that our life on Earth is temporary. What do you want your life to count for?

LINE IT UP!

Plant some wake-up calls for yourself. Pick a few of your favorite verses from this week's lesson and write each one on a small piece of paper. Put them in drawers at home or in your book bag or school locker—anyplace you'll find them unexpectedly one day. Whenever you find one, hide it somewhere else to find again. They'll come as a surprise to help keep your mind focused on being a success in God's eyes.

PRAYER POWER

Do you want to be successful God's way? Commit today's activities, as well your future plans, to him. He has something special in mind for your life. Ask him to prepare you for that and to guide you each day. God bless!

WEEK 8

WHAT'S UP THIS WEEK:
Respecting the Rules

THEME VERSES FOR THE WEEK:
Proverbs 1:22-33

How long will you go on being simpleminded?
How long will you mockers relish your mocking? How long will you fools fight the facts?
Come here and listen to me! I'll pour out the
spirit of wisdom upon you and make you wise.
I called you so often, but you didn't come. I
reached out to you, but you paid no attention.
You ignored my advice and rejected the correc-
tion I offered. . . . For they hated knowledge
and chose not to fear the Lord. They rejected
my advice and paid no attention when I cor-
rected them. That is why they must eat the
bitter fruit of living their own way. They must
experience the full terror of the path they
have chosen. For they are simpletons who

turn away from me—to death. They are fools, and their own complacency will destroy them. But all who listen to me will live in peace and safety, unafraid of harm.

A beautiful day on the water, warm skies, diving gear sitting nearby . . . but only one diver. The rules say not to dive alone. But how important are rules for an experienced diver? Mike is about to find out.

Blow Out

"Are you sure you should do this?" my 13-year-old brother, Joey, asked. He was standing at the back of the boat. Far beyond him, I saw the Florida shoreline, a dark smudge against the bright blue sky.

Standing at the front of the boat and ready to jump into the water with full scuba gear, I rolled my eyes.

"Look, kid," I said. "Rules are for people who need them to feel safe. Smart people know when to break the rules. I'm smart and this is one of those times. It's not our fault that Larry decided to go to church for the first time in his life."

My friend Larry—or maybe I should call him an ex-friend—had called me last night and jammed out of this morning's dive. I'd told him we had planned this all week and needed three people—one for the boat and two to dive together. Larry had said we could wait for the afternoon. I told him to forget that, it was supposed to be an all-day dive. Larry had asked if maybe I was still mad about this whole church thing. I had told him that yeah, I was—church was a bunch of rules, and smart people didn't need to be told what to do.

Out here on the water, I repeated all of this to Joey. I was his older, tougher brother. Joey wasn't about to see me chicken out of a dive because some stupid friend was suddenly interested in believing in God.

"You know how to handle the boat," I finished to Joey. "Keep it from drifting. I'll be up in half an hour. Who knows, we could be rich by then."

With a big grin, I put my mask over my head and jumped backwards into the water.

Diving alone scares other people, but not me. I'm 18, and I'd spent every afternoon of my entire life around these waters. I had gone diving a thousand times and not once had anything gone wrong. A lot of that time I'd spent looking for things you could find in wrecked pirate ships—like the one that was waiting for me 90 feet below.

I kicked my fins and swam down 10 feet. Slowly. Since I was diving alone—without Larry—it was time to be extra smart and careful.

At 40 feet deep, I turned my head and watched for sharks. Especially hammerheads. Around Key Largo, they can be as long as a car. But much more dangerous. Cars just need gasoline for fuel. Sharks need meat and blood. I didn't want to be a quick fill-up for a shark.

I saw no sharks. There were plenty of smaller fish. Although I knew they were very colorful, they looked bluish grey. Even clear water soaks up colors. After 50 feet, reds and oranges and yellows are gone. The blue colors go after 60 feet.

At 70 feet deep, I checked the dial on my air tank. It showed full. I had only been in the water for 15 minutes. Plenty of time left. Plenty of air.

At 75 feet, I stopped to plug my nose through my dive mask. I swallowed hard and popped my ears, something I had been doing all the way down. This helps keep your eardrums from exploding.

I finally reached the shipwreck at 90 feet. This ship had gone down in a storm in the late 1700s. A lot of scuba divers had gone through it during the years, but there was always the chance I might find something valuable, like an old compass or a broken sword. Besides, scuba diving was so much fun, I didn't need much of an excuse to go down.

I'd been at the wreck plenty of times. I knew the best way in—a jagged hole in the side of the ship. I turned on my flashlight and started in.

Only, just as half of my body was inside the ship, a shark's head appeared!

Its mouth was open wide and rows of sharp teeth showed shiny white in my flashlight beam.

I pushed back. And banged my scuba tank against the hull of the ship. I was stuck.

The shark lunged forward toward me.

I did the only thing I could. I bashed the shark on the nose with my flashlight.

It worked! The five-foot monster turned around and disappeared into the darkness of the wreck.

Which left me alone and stuck.

I spun my back and tried to twist loose.

Nothing.

I tried the other way, yanking twice as hard. The water around me exploded with bubbles! My twisting and turning must have pulled my air hose loose from the base of my scuba tank!

Now I was free, but I needed air. Badly. And soon. I was 93 feet underwater.

I tried to stay calm. In scuba diving, if you stop thinking, you're in trouble.

I knew I had two problems. One problem, of course, was needing air. There was lots of it above the water. But I'd have to swim 90 feet straight up to get to it.

Except it wouldn't be that easy. And that was my other problem. If I didn't do it right, my lungs would explode. There was a simple reason for it. The deeper you go, the more the weight of the water squeezes things. Including air.

Once, I had shown Joey exactly how it worked. I had taken him 33 feet underwater with an empty plastic milk jug. I had filled it with air and taken Joey and the milk jug deeper. As we had continued down, water pressure squeezed the jug. It looked like an invisible hand was crushing it. At 66 feet deep, the jug was half the size it had been.

It worked the same way in reverse. As you rose there was less weight and the water squeezed less, so the same amount of air would take more space.

At 66 feet deep I had added air from my scuba tank to the crushed jug, filling it until it was normal size again. As Joey and I swam up again, the air in the jug pushed out because there was less water pressure squeezing it. It was like watching someone blow up a balloon. Back at 33 feet, the air inside had expanded so much that the plastic jug ripped wide open.

That's what would happen to my lungs if I swam up too quickly. The air now inside my lungs would expand as I rose. Fifty feet up from the pirate ship, my lungs would explode like the milk jug.

And I had 90 feet before I reached the surface.

There was only one thing to do: breathe out the whole time I swam upward.

I dropped the weights from my belt and pushed away from the ship. I kicked upward. Already I wanted to suck for air. But I forced myself to breathe out, not in. I absolutely had to blow air out of my lungs so that they wouldn't explode like the plastic milk jug.

I kicked more. It got easier. Without the weights, I was like a cork. I kept pushing air out of my lungs. My body screamed at me for it. It wanted all the air it could get. But if I held my breath, my lungs would rip.

Higher and higher. Second after second. I kept breathing out, kept pushing air out of my starving lungs.

Just like a cork, I began moving faster and faster. There was still air in my diving vest from where I had pumped it in on my way down. That air was taking me higher and faster.

My sight became fuzzy black around the edges. I needed air so badly I was about to pass out. But if I did, my body would try to breathe. My lungs would suck in water, not air.

"Dear God," I prayed, "help me, help me, help me."

I kept praying those words. It took my mind off the burning pain in my lungs. Would I make it to the surface in time?

Just as total blackness began to close in, I popped into the air.

I fell back into the water. As I paddled, I sucked in lungfuls of sweet life.

"Mike!" Joey called. "You okay?"

All I could do was nod as I gasped and blew air.

Joey began to power the boat toward me.

"What happened?" he said as he got closer.

I thought about it without answering. I'd gone diving alone

and nearly paid for my mistake with my life. Next time, I wouldn't be so quick to think rules were dumb.

Then I realized something else. Why, when death was so close, had I prayed and prayed and prayed? Could it be that church was more than rules? I decided right there to ask Larry more about it when I saw him.

Joey reached out with a pole. I grabbed it and let him pull me toward the boat. I was still so weak I could barely hold on.

When I rolled into the boat, I told Joey about bashing the shark on the nose.

"Wow," he said. "Good thing you outsmarted it."

"Yeah," I said. "But there's not a whole lot smart about me. I'm learning, though."

WHAT'S UP THIS WEEK?

- Why the Rules?
- Knowing We Don't Know It All
- Fearing God

PRAYER POWER

Rules may not be anyone's favorite topic to talk about, but they're important. Why not start the week out right by asking God to guide your attitude and views about living by the rules?

WHY THE RULES?

Why are there so many rules, and why do we need them? Those are very important questions. Sometimes it can seem as though everyone's out there wanting to set limitations on us and trying to fence us in. It's easier to go by the rules when we understand why they were created in the first place. That's what we'll look into today.

BRAIN STRETCHERS

FOR KIDS:

1. In "Blow Out," Mike thinks that rules are dumb. How does his mind change?
2. What did he learn about rules?
3. What rules in your house do you least like following? Why do you think those are important?

ASK AN ADULT:

1. Is it sometimes hard for you to follow rules?
2. What rules in the Bible do you least like following? What do you do when you don't like a rule?

SCRIPTURE POWER

And now, Israel, listen carefully to these laws and regulations that I am about to teach you. Obey them so that you may live, so you may enter and occupy the land the Lord, the God of your ancestors, is giving you.' . . . You must obey these laws and regulations when you arrive in the land you are about to enter and occupy. The Lord my God gave them to me and commanded me to pass them on to you. If you obey them carefully, you will display your wisdom and intelligence to the surrounding nations. When they hear about these laws, they will exclaim, "What other nation is as wise and prudent as this!" For what great nation has a god as near to them as the Lord our God is near to us whenever we call on him? (Deuteronomy 4:1, 5-7)

Rules, rules, rules. Rules have been around for a very long time. God gave his nation of Israel a list of rules and explained his purpose for them and the good things that would happen if the people obeyed.

If you obey all the laws and commands that I will give you today, all will be well with you and your children. Then you will enjoy a long life in the land the Lord your God is giving you for all time. (Deuteronomy 4:40)

Whether we love 'em or hate 'em, rules provide necessary boundaries and protection to help keep our life on the right track. Nobody likes to be bossed around. Rules are made to be broken, right? When we see God's Word as a set of rules, we miss out on a very key element: God loves us! The direction he has set for our life is there for our protection because he doesn't want to see us get hurt.

> *Wisdom will multiply your days and add years to your life. If you become wise, you will be the one to benefit. If you scorn wisdom, you will be the one to suffer. (Proverbs 9:11-12)*

Obeying rules shows wisdom on our part. Rules are a little bit like a bicycle helmet. We may not like how the helmet looks and feels, and we might rather ride with the wind blowing our hair back, truly free. But when we hit a pothole and are sent flying, the helmet suddenly makes sense. We may get a little banged up, but the helmet we despised before could be the very thing that saves our life.

You may not really like rules, and you may wish you could do what you wanted all the time. But when a tough situation comes up, those rules can save you from disaster!

PRAYER POWER

What do you think of rules in general? God wants to work with you where you are. Tell him what you think, but be open to his power to change you. He can help you see things his way. It's the only way to truly live life to its fullest.

KNOWING WE DON'T KNOW IT ALL

Sometimes it seems that no one else is quite as smart as we are. If we're honest, we've all probably felt that way once or twice, right? One sign of intelligence, however, is being able to admit our limitations. We don't have all the answers. That's what we'll talk about today.

BRAIN STRETCHERS

FOR KIDS:

1. What's wrong with Mike's attitude in "Blow Out"? Does he think he knows it all?
2. What could have happened to him in the story?
3. Are you ever tempted to think you know it all?

ASK AN ADULT:

1. Do you ever feel like you know it all?
2. Has there ever been a time when you put yourself or someone else in danger because of a dumb decision like Mike's? What happened?

SCRIPTURE POWER

Not even the wisest people know everything, even if they say they do. (Ecclesiastes 8:17)

This verse was written by King Solomon, who was known for being incredibly wise. Looks like he learned a thing or two about knowing it all.

Fear of the Lord is the beginning of knowledge. Only fools despise wisdom and discipline. (Proverbs 1:7)

King Solomon also wrote this verse. He knew how foolish it is to think we don't need the wisdom and discipline of rules. By "fear of the Lord," he didn't mean being scared of God. He simply meant having a genuine respect, or reverence, for God. Obeying God is the first step toward being a wise person.

My child, listen to me and treasure my instructions. Tune your ears to wisdom, and concentrate on understanding. Cry out for insight and understanding. Search for them as you would for lost money or hidden treasure. Then you will understand what it means to fear the Lord, and you will gain knowledge of God. For the Lord grants wisdom! From his mouth come knowledge and understanding. He grants a treasure of good sense to the godly. He is their shield, protecting those who walk with integrity. He guards the paths of justice and protects those who are faithful to him. (Proverbs 2:1-8)

Here's some more info about what it means to fear God and gain understanding and wisdom for living life. From these verses, we get the idea that treasuring God's instructions brings understanding, good sense, and protection—all things we need to live successfully.

I believe in your commands; now teach me good judgment and knowledge. . . . You made me; you created me. Now give me the sense to follow your commands. (Psalm 119:66, 73)

We all have room to grow in wisdom and learn to abide by rules. We can't do it on our own, which is the whole point. We can only do it by accepting salvation and walking daily in the strength of Jesus, rather than trying to accomplish it on our own.

PRAYER POWER

How's your attitude as far as being able to admit you need rules? If there's room for improvement, ask God to help you with it. He'll be pleased with your humble attitude.

FEARING GOD

Yesterday we touched on fearing God, or having a healthy respect for his authority and rightful place as ruler of the universe. That's worth talking about more today.

BRAIN STRETCHERS
FOR KIDS:
1. Why do you think God gives us rules to live by?
2. How do you think God feels when we disobey?
3. How does it make you feel to know that we hurt God when we sin?

ASK AN ADULT:
1. Can you think of some rules God gave that you're glad to know? Why or why not?
2. Sometimes it's tempting to disobey rules that don't seem as important as others. Why should we obey rules if we know we won't get hurt by disobeying them?

SCRIPTURE POWER

Fear of the Lord is a life-giving fountain; it offers escape from the snares of death. (Proverbs 14:27)

Fear of the Lord gives life, security, and protection from harm. (Proverbs 19:23)

The law of the Lord is perfect, reviving the soul. The decrees of the Lord are trustworthy, making wise the simple. (Psalm 19:7)

God's laws are for our protection, and he loves us so much that he wants only the best for us. His teachings are not just good; they're perfect! We can't achieve perfection here on Earth, but God has given us teachings and laws to live by which are flawless and will keep us from harm and give us a fulfilling life. Now we need to trust God and ask for his help to follow these teachings each day.

Your word is a lamp for my feet and a light for my path. (Psalm 119:105)

It is difficult to walk on a path in darkness. We trip on stones and branches, and the journey can really beat us up. It can get pretty scary, too, since we can't see where we're going and often end up getting lost. It's a lot easier to walk with a flashlight. God's commands are like a great beam of light, which shines on our path and helps us to avoid the snares and pitfalls. His laws keep us from falling.

God has called us to be holy, not to live impure lives. Anyone who refuses to live by these rules is not disobeying human rules but is rejecting God, who gives his Holy Spirit to you. (1 Thessalonians 4:7-8)

There's a bigger picture here when it comes to obeying those in authority who make the rules. When Mike refused to obey the rules about not diving alone, he was rejecting God's authority. His mocking attitude made it obvious that he didn't care about pleasing God. But God was merciful and used a seriously dangerous situation to change Mike's attitude.

Oh, the joys of those who do not follow the advice of the wicked, or stand around with sinners, or join in with scoffers. But they delight in doing everything the Lord wants; day and night they think about his law. They are like trees planted along the riverbank, bearing fruit each season without fail. Their leaves never wither, and in all they do, they prosper. (Psalm 1:1-3)

Following God's laws can seem like an impossible task, and we can get discouraged. We need to get our eyes off of what we can't do and focus on what we *can* do. God wants us to include him in every part of our life. When we do, we become strong trees that produce fruit.

I lavish my love on those who love me and obey my commands, even for a thousand generations. (Deuteronomy 5:10)

You will be blessed if you obey the commands of the Lord your God that I am giving you today. (Deuteronomy 11:27)

God promises great rewards for those who keep his laws! Remember: Obedience always brings blessing.

PRAYER POWER

Ask God today to help you have a healthy fear of him. Spend a few moments telling him why you respect him and that you want to obey the people in authority over you in order to please him.

CONCLUDING THOUGHTS

In "Blow Out," Mike found out that he's not as smart as he thought he was. In diving, there are safety rules to follow, which are there for a reason: safety! Mike had done so much diving in his life without any problems that he was sure he'd be fine. Most of the time, nothing bad would have happened, but the safety rules are there for the one-in-a-thousand time when something goes wrong. Mike found himself in trouble because he didn't respect the rules—or God.

Maybe the day will come when you'll face a life-threatening situation like Mike did. Decide now how you're going to live—following the rules or breaking them. Give God the opportunity to help you grow in strength to keep respecting his authority.

Remember: Obedience always brings blessing.

LINE IT UP!

With your family or Bible study group, talk about the story from Joey's point of view. He may have looked up to his older brother, Mike. How might Mike's decision to disobey the rules have affected Joey? Discuss whether or not Mike was a good role model for Joey. Then talk to the people in your lives who are influenced by watching you. Apologize for the times when you haven't been a good role model.

PRAYER POWER

It's been a big week talking about rules. Pray that God will help you understand more and more the importance of living by his rules. Ask him to help you want to obey him more. Then thank him ahead of time for the blessings he's sure to send your way when you follow his rules.

WHAT'S UP THIS WEEK:
God's Kind of Love

THEME VERSE FOR THE WEEK:
2 Thessalonians 3:5

May the Lord bring you into an ever deeper
understanding of the love of God.

Sometimes love appears in unexpected ways. In "The Sweater," Robert learns an important lesson about love at its best.

The Sweater

"Pssst!"

I ignored the cow beside me and looked through my eyeholes at the audience in our school gym to see why the old lady in the front row had her head so stooped.

"Pssssssst!"

I gave up on the lady, tilted my head sideways, and squinted at the floor. Since I wasn't standing on its tail, what could this dumb cow want?

"Pssssssssssst!"

Finally, I gave in. If I didn't, this cow would get louder than the two horses talking beside the manger.

"What is it?" I hissed.

"Mummbble. Mummbble. Mummbble."

Donkey costumes will do that to you—block your hearing. It's also hot and sweaty inside. Worse, your eyeholes keep shifting position and make it next to impossible to see.

"What?!?" Even though my best

friend, Fred, was equally suffocated in his cow costume, I'm sure he heard my grumpiness. Donkey costumes will also do that to a person.

The cow's nose bumped against my ear. A low voice filtered through my donkey ears. "I said, 'Robert, where did your uncle get the hay for the manger?' "

"From his—." My eyeholes shifted enough for me to notice Mr. Berthude, our drama teacher, glaring in our direction from the side of the stage.

"—farm," I finished in a lower voice.

"Well, I think I just saw a *ooof!*"

I moved my heel over his toes and crunched downward. We did not need the full wrath of Mr. Berthude, a tall and skinny man who wore black suits and smiled only when he was handing out demerits or after-school detentions.

For this Christmas play, Mr. Berthude had repeatedly stressed that donations from the audience would raise money for a planned addition to a nearby senior citizens' home, with those seniors as special guests in the three front rows.

"The birth is a miracle from God," one horse said before Fred recovered.

"Yes," the other answered. "Come all, and view the baby!"

That was our cue to edge forward. That's when I was finally able to see what the old lady was doing with her head bent so far over.

She was knitting.

My job at this point was to admire the baby doll in the manger, but I couldn't help staring at the old lady from behind my eyeholes.

She hadn't looked up once since our arrival. Not during

the introductions. Not during our Christmas carols. Not now during the nativity scene.

That bothered me. We'd practiced a lot for tonight, everyone else seemed to be enjoying us, and her sweater seemed nearly finished.

I stole another glance and almost snorted. It wasn't like she would finish tonight anyway. She was so slow that watching her knit made my own hands hurt. Her old, old fingers were skinny and knotted like chicken bones, curled almost into a ball. She could barely move the needles.

With her head down, intent on knitting, she was missing a good play, too. Along with us talking animals, we would have actual flying angels. Plus, tons of work had gone into making the scenery perfect. My uncle, in fact, had not only pitchforked huge clumps of straw into the manger but had spread the rest of a truckload all across the stage.

"Surely this is no ordinary human child," Fred said.

"Hark, do I hear herald angels sing?" I asked. I wanted to shout at the old lady and tell her to pay attention.

Ooohing from the audience told me that the angels were making their grand entrance above me.

Did the old lady at least enjoy the sight of the angels swooping down on invisible wires attached to the belts that suspended them in the air?

No reaction from her at all. She just kept knitting. I wanted to reach out and break those stupid knitting needles.

My eye caught movement in the manger straw.

No way, I told myself. But two small grey furry objects scooted to the other side of the manger.

Mice! Fred had tried to tell me that he thought he'd seen mice!

I remembered visits to my uncle's farm and the constant

rustling in the straw of the barn. My uncle, no doubt, had accidently scooped mice along with all the straw. A thought chilled me: How would the girls handle this, sissies as they were? Hah! A mouse would probably send them screaming into . . .

What had just touched my ankle?

I froze.

What was now moving up my leg?

I told myself it was my imagination.

"Peace on Earth to all men," Fred said.

Tiny claws dug hard into my skin. It *was* a mouse.

"Yaaarggh!" I said in reply to Fred.

"Idiot," Fred hissed. "Ask the angels to sing."

The mouse scurried even higher on my body.

"Yaaaargggh!" I spun in panic and ran around the manger as I hopped and shook my leg.

In the darkness of my costume, I slammed into two shepherds who had moved into position to sing with us animals. They fell into the manger, which crashed into the cow and horses, who toppled onto their big noses, just as the baby doll from the manger flew over them. Not once had I stopped screaming.

Finally, I, too, fell into the confusion. On my back, I could see that the angels hung motionless as they stared downward in horror.

The entire gym was filled with shocked silence, until that stupid mouse decided to run out from the bottom of my costume to dart a couple of laps in the center of the stage before disappearing into some nearby straw.

That's when the laughter began in a low rumble and became deafening thunder.

When I was able to stand, I happened to look at the lady who knitted. I saw even she had stopped and had a smile on her face. But almost right away she got serious again and began to knit, just as slowly as before.

What would it take to get this inconsiderate person's attention?

It seemed like hours until we were sorted out. The scenery was wrecked so badly and everyone was howling so loudly with laughter, there was no sense in trying to continue.

Mr. Berthude told us to bow for a standing ovation. He couldn't stay mad for long, not when donations at the end were three times as much as expected.

▼ ▼ ▼ ▼ ▼

Mrs. Henry, a next-door neighbor and one of the directors of the senior citizens' home, stopped by as we were clearing the gymnasium.

"You shouldn't feel bad, Robert," she said. "It was a wonderful Christmas program, anyway. All of us enjoyed it."

"What about the lady who likes knitting better than all of our hard work?" I asked. "It looked to me like her sweater was nearly finished anyway."

The tone of my voice must have told her what I thought about the lady's rudeness.

Mrs. Henry studied my face before she spoke.

"Oh, you noticed. That's Emma Byrd."

She thought for a second and then continued. "You're out of school on Christmas Eve. Why don't you stop by? You'll understand better then."

▼ ▼ ▼ ▼ ▼

A week later, Mrs. Henry took me to old Emma Byrd, who was sitting almost underneath the branches of a Christmas tree. She looked tiny beside all the decorations.

"Hello, young man," she said. "Mrs. Henry tells me you are the one delivering my package this year."

I was?

"Thank you very much." She smiled and then gazed far away, lost in her private memories.

I guess I was delivering it.

Mrs. Henry led me away and she handed me a carefully wrapped package.

"This is the sweater," she said. "Emma has bad arthritis. The last part of the sleeve took her all this week. She was determined to finish it before Christmas."

"All week?" I asked. "Just for part of a sleeve?"

Mrs. Henry nodded. "The sweater took a lot of love and exactly one year to make."

"Exactly a year," I said slowly. "That means she started last . . ."

Mrs. Henry nodded. " . . . Christmas. Emma's favorite day. She says that baby Jesus is the miracle that starts everything for us, so that's the day she starts on something she can give in celebration, a task that will remind her of the miracle every day of the year."

Oh. And I'd wanted to break her needles during the play.

Mrs. Henry smiled gently at my reaction. "Unfortunately, Emma's hands are getting worse, Robert. This year Emma worried she might not finish in time. That's why she couldn't stop during the Christmas play."

"Oh."

"Anyway," Mrs. Henry finished, "I promised her that you would find the right person for her gift. Is that okay with you?"

I nodded. It was all I could manage as I thought of the sacrifice it had taken to make that sweater, and how I'd worried more about being appreciated than about what Christmas meant.

I didn't deliver the sweater immediately. Instead, I hurried home, took all of my rainy-day money, and bought an armful of presents for Santas Anonymous to deliver Christmas morning. Those presents, I figured, would share as much of Emma's celebration as possible, and they just might be fair payment for what I planned to do with her sweater.

Because the next morning, I gave that sweater to myself. Who would appreciate it more than I would every Christmas, even if it didn't fit and one sleeve was longer than the other?

WHAT'S UP THIS WEEK?
- Love Is . . .
- God Loved First
- Love in Action

PRAYER POWER
As you pray today, ask God to show you new truths about himself and the way he loves. He will bless your desire to be more like him.

LOVE IS . . .

If we stop to think about it, most of us hear the word *love* at least once a day. It's easy to toss it around casually, as if it's something that comes and goes. Let's find out how God defines love.

BRAIN STRETCHERS

FOR KIDS:

1. What is love?
2. In "The Sweater," Robert jumped to some conclusions about Emma Byrd without knowing her or the reasons for her actions. What did Robert end up learning about love from her?

ASK AN ADULT:

1. What's the difference between loving things and loving people?
2. Is there a difference between liking someone and loving that person?

SCRIPTURE POWER

This is real love. It is not that we loved God, but that he loved us and sent his Son as a sacrifice to take away our sins. (1 John 4:10)

Love is costly. Jesus gave his life out of his love for us. Kind of makes a person think twice about saying the word *love* without really meaning it, huh? We use the word *love* carelessly, not doing it justice. We love football, ice cream, sleeping in, and summer holidays. But we also love our family and God— hopefully in a deeper way. It's easy to see how the word gets watered down when we use it so frequently—and more often than not for trivial things.

> God is love, and all who live in love live in God, and God lives in them. And as we live in God, our love grows more perfect. (1 John 4:16-17)

Love is a little word with a whole lotta power. Love's main goal is the good of the one being loved. It puts other people first. When we are filled with God's love, we can pour ourselves into others without expecting something in return. Through Christ, we can have compassion for others, seeing their needs and longing to help fill them.

> Love is patient and kind. Love is not jealous or boastful or proud or rude. Love does not demand its own way. Love is not irritable, and it keeps no record of when it has been wronged. It is never glad about injustice but rejoices whenever the truth wins out. (1 Corinthians 13:4-6)

Love is considerate. It treats others well. It's forgiving and unselfish, and it gives others a chance without judging them. Robert made the mistake of getting irritated by what seemed like rudeness from Emma. In reality, she was showing more love than he was.

PRAYER POWER

We're still at the beginning of the week, and there is a lot to learn about love. When you pray each day, really focus your mind and your heart on God and what he wants to help you understand about love.

GOD LOVED FIRST

In order to better understand the meaning of love, we need to figure out where love began. Who thought of it? You guessed it. God is the creator of love.

BRAIN STRETCHERS
FOR KIDS:

1. In "The Sweater," how does Emma Byrd show her love? Why do you think she does that?
2. How do your parents show that they love you? How does God show his love for you?

ASK AN ADULT:

1. Why do so many people say they love something or someone without showing it through their actions?
2. What's the difference between the world's love and God's love?

SCRIPTURE POWER

God showed how much he loved us by sending his only Son into the world so that we might have eternal life through him. (1 John 4:9)

God has always been a loving God. But his greatest gift of love was when he paid the ultimate price to save us. He gave his Son, Jesus, to die in our place. We can have eternal life only because of that gift. Think about that for a minute. If you've accepted Jesus as your Savior, then you're going to heaven. Imagine if Jesus had never died. If that were the case, then no one would be going to heaven. God's love is amazing and powerful.

> *See how very much our heavenly Father loves us, for he allows us to be called his children, and we really are! (1 John 3:1)*

Think about how much parents love their kids. When Jesus died for us, God gave us the right to be part of his family as his children. Most parents would do anything to keep their kids safe and provide for their needs. God did *everything* to save us. We're his kids, and he loves us perfectly and for always.

> *We love each other as a result of his loving us first. (1 John 4:19)*

It is impossible to measure how much God loves us. As we allow ourselves to be filled with God's love, it will spill over to those around us. As we know God better, we will want to love others better.

PRAYER POWER

Ask God today to help you be aware of all the ways he shows his love for you. Thank him for his love, and ask him to help you learn from his example.

LOVE IN ACTION

It's easy to say we love someone or to think of ourselves as loving people. But how good are we at really showing our love? Are we unselfish, putting the needs and feelings of others before our own? Let's dig deeper into this today.

BRAIN STRETCHERS

FOR KIDS:

1. In "The Sweater," how does Robert attempt to love his neighbor at the story's end?
2. What makes you feel loved? What things do you do to show people you love them?
3. How much do you love yourself? How should you treat your family, based on the idea of loving your neighbor as yourself? What are some things you could do better to show your love?

ASK AN ADULT:

1. Have you ever chosen to love someone when you didn't feel like it? How did you do it?
2. What are some things you do to show you love your family?

3. When is it hard for you to think of actions that will show your love?

SCRIPTURE POWER

Love never gives up, never loses faith, is always hopeful, and endures through every circumstance. (1 Corinthians 13:7)

Love is a verb—an action word. Love requires courage and determination, strength and unselfishness. It's a word for heroes. Read the above verse again with these thoughts in mind. The ability to love like that on a daily basis comes only from God.

The most important piece of clothing you must wear is love. Love is what binds us all together in perfect harmony. (Colossians 3:14)

Love is like glue; it helps people stick together. As Christians, we need to treat others differently than the world treats people. There are many important things to remember when relating to others, but love is the biggest. When we put on love, the other issues become smaller.

If someone says, "I love God," but hates a Christian brother or sister, that person is a liar; for if we don't love people we can see, how can we love God, whom we have not seen? And God himself has commanded that we must love not only him but our Christian brothers and sisters, too. (1 John 4:20-21)

The Christian life should be different from that of nonbelievers. We are expected to treat each other differently, because

God has changed our heart and redeemed our life. We must continue to grow closer to the One who saved us, becoming more and more like him in the way we love.

The whole law can be summed up in this one command: "Love your neighbor as yourself." (Galatians 5:14)

Selfishness causes us to grab for whatever we can get, without thought for how it might hurt others. True love considers the needs and desires of others and longs for the best for other people. This kind of love is only possible with God's help. We must make a choice to love each other, rather than focusing on our selfish desires. It's easy to speak of love, but actions speak much more loudly than words.

PRAYER POWER

Okay, after looking at what God's Word says about love in action, are there any ways you could improve the way you show love to others? Today would be a great day to thank God for all the ways he shows you his love.

CONCLUDING THOUGHTS

In "The Sweater," Robert takes his part as a donkey in the Christmas program very seriously. Their drama class has worked hard to make sure that everything will go well. Robert wants the audience to enjoy and appreciate the play, and he doesn't want Mr. Berthude to be angry with their class. It doesn't seem right, then, that a little old lady sitting at the front should ignore the play and be engrossed in knitting, after all the effort the drama class has put in.

When Robert finds out the reason Emma Byrd was knitting during the Christmas program, he is struck by her love and compassion. She sacrificed all year long to make a sweater as a gift of celebration of Christ's love. Her example of love is one that Robert will never forget, and he's got a sweater as a constant reminder.

LINE IT UP!

Time for a brainstorm session. See how long a list your family or Bible study friends can come up with for as many of these categories as you want:

- All the ways God shows you he loves you
- Qualities you love about God
- Ways you can show love to others
- Things others do that make you feel loved

PRAYER POWER

What did you learn this week about love? Talk to God about it. Spend your prayer time today thanking God again for his love. And remind yourself each day that you can love because you are loved!

WHAT'S UP THIS WEEK:
More on Love

THEME VERSE FOR THE WEEK:
Ephesians 5:2

Live a life filled with love for others, following the example of Christ, who loved you and gave himself as a sacrifice to take away your sins.

It was just a simple joke, right? She was just a crabby old lady who made their lives miserable every Sunday. Ricky and Hummer are about to discover that there's more to people than meets the eye.

Church Lady

Here's advice you can have for free: Leave dead skunks where they belong— on the side of the road.

It was advice I repeated to Hummer.

"Give me a break," she said, jabbing my chest with her forefinger to empha- size each word, something she does as much as possible to prove how tough she is.

"It's dark," I pointed out unnecessar- ily. If the dead skunk heaped on the ground beside us didn't smell so bad, we never would have found it on our return. A country road like this has no lights. Lots of strange rustlings in the trees along the road, but no lights.

"It's also cold," I continued above the wind and what I hoped was only the rustling of dry leaves. "No matter *what* day it is, dead skunks don't make me happy."

I didn't point out that I was also scared of what she had planned. It's not smart to let Hummer know how tough she actually is.

"Why not?" she challenged. "Scared?"

Hummer and her mom have been my next-door neighbors for as long as I can remember. Which means by now she can read my mind.

"Well, I'd rather be in a pirate's costume getting bagfuls of candy."

Hummer snorted. "Ricky, don't you think 13's a little old for that kind of begging?" She paused, then she imitated the kids we'd heard going door-to-door on our way out of town. "Trick or treat! Trick or treat!" Then she spit. "Bah. Treats just rot your teeth. But tricks, those are too cool."

Hummer is not only tough but stubborn—and determined to do whatever she pleases whether people like it or not. Trying to stop her is like trying to stop a thunderstorm.

I think it's because she wants to prove to the whole world that it doesn't matter to her that her dad ran away when she was a baby. And that it doesn't matter that everybody knows about the envelope with no return address that her mother gets once a week with cash inside from someone in town who understands how badly they've always needed money.

I can't prove my theory, though. I only asked once about the money, and in reply Hummer caught me with a punch so fast even she didn't know it would happen. She cried and apologized while I bled from my nose and apologized, and neither of us ever mentioned her dad or the money gift again.

She hummed now as I fumbled to get my flashlight from my knapsack. "Too cool," Hummer repeated softly between tunes. "A dead-skunk trick is too cool."

What could I say? Especially since too much of this had been my idea. Of course, at the time—barely four hours ago—I'd just been joking.

▼ ▼ ▼ ▼ ▼

Hummer and I had been in the backseat of the car on the trip back from visiting my grandmother, who lives a few miles out of town. Mom was behind the wheel, gritting her teeth at every car that passed, when all of us groaned at the stench that suddenly filled our nostrils.

"Could you speed up just a little, Mrs. Kidd?" Hummer gagged and pleaded. "That skunk must have sprayed the entire county before it died."

"It was someone going too fast who killed that poor creature in the first place," Mom said. "And I never take chances with Joel asleep here in the front."

On cue, my six-year-old little brother woke up, plugged his nose, and started to gag. Under cover of that noise, I whispered to Hummer, "My feelings exactly. Imagine waking up to a smell like that."

Hummer stopped plugging her own nose to stare at me in thought. Then she grinned. "Imagine that," she said. "Just imagine that."

So now it was two hours after supper and we were back at the same spot three miles from the edge of town. Hummer was equipped with rubber gloves and I had a huge plastic bag, and we were ready to disregard my advice about leaving dead skunks where they belonged.

The only thing that made me feel better was that Hummer lost the coin toss and had to be the one to carry the skunk back to town.

189

▼ ▼ ▼ ▼ ▼

"Ricky, for the last time, this is foolproof. Didn't your mom mention that Old Lady Lutz won't be back until tomorrow afternoon?" Hummer hummed some more. Which is why she had that nickname. Whenever she was impatient—almost always—she hummed. Just like some people drum their fingers or tap their feet.

Foolproof or not, I didn't like this. In fact, I knew it was wrong. But it was like being on the ridge of a slippery roof. One little wrong step puts you on the slope, and you don't stop the next little step, and all of a sudden you're sliding out of control and just about off the edge of the roof.

Same with this. You make a half joke about something, and then you laugh when Hummer takes it further with a plan that sounds funny, and you work it out just in theory, and suddenly it seems like there never was a good time to say no. And there you are in front of Old Lady Lutz's house waiting for the lights to go off in the house across the street so that you can deliver a dead skunk.

I voiced those doubts aloud.

"Foolproof or not, this might be too much," I whispered.

"To an old skinflint like her? I mean, she's the crabbiest Sunday school teacher we've ever had."

"Well . . . " It *was* true, though. Old Lady Lutz was quick to scold and give us the evil eye anytime we stopped paying attention. She was one part of church I didn't really like.

Hummer began jabbing her finger in my chest again. "Besides, doesn't your Dad crack up like crazy when he tells you about some of the Halloween stunts his uncles pulled when they were growing up?"

In the moonlight, Hummer's short blonde hair looked silver.

I pushed her finger aside. "Well . . . "

"How about when they moved your great-granddad's out-house back a few feet?" she asked. "And when he walked up to it in the middle of the night he—"

"Fine, fine," I said quickly. "Let's just get this over with."

And at that moment, the front hall light across the street silently clicked off. The rest of the lights followed, and within moments, the shadows around us were deep enough for action.

Hummer stopped humming.

"Now's the time, bud!"

She grabbed my arm and dragged me to Old Lady Lutz's mailbox, stuck on a post at the edge of the street where the mailman could reach it easily.

She looked quickly in both directions.

"Ricky, open it!"

I sighed and opened it.

She pulled the plastic bag from her knapsack and pushed it inside, then peeled the plastic back from the dead skunk. It was difficult not to gag at the stench.

"Done!" she said. She carefully folded the plastic and placed that and her rubber gloves inside another plastic bag.

I noticed the little red flag on the mailbox pointing up, tell-ing the mailman there were letters waiting to be posted.

"Hummer, there was mail in there."

Hummer shrugged. "Then Happy Halloween for the mail-man, too."

▼ ▼ ▼ ▼ ▼

It was the talk of the school for two days: How the mail-man—who had a bad cold and couldn't smell a thing—had reached in and grabbed the letters and the skunk at the same

191

time. How after she got home Old Lady Lutz had calmly chopped the mailbox down and burned it among her raked fall leaves. How nobody could figure out who had played such a cool Halloween trick.

After school on the second day, I stopped by Hummer's house. She was in the backyard in the middle of a mess of tools and pieces of wood of all shapes and sizes.

"Hummer," I shouted. "What's this mess? You building a house or something?"

"Yeah, whatever," she looked up and answered with a shrug. Then she added quietly, "I am building something. It's a mailbox. At least, it will be a mailbox."

She looked at me as confusion must have clouded my face. That's when I noticed the tears in her eyes.

"Hummer . . . " I began.

"Don't," she warned me. "Don't even ask."

I didn't. Instead, I gradually noticed a smell. *Skunk*.

"Hummer?"

"I said not to ask."

Then she reached in her back pocket and pulled out an envelope, which she handed to me. It had no return address, and through its ripped corner, I could see the edges of some 10-dollar bills.

Hummer had her back to me as she reached for her tape measure. I pulled the envelope free and brought it close to my face.

My eyes watered. *Skunk*.

Then I understood. *Through rain or snow . . .*

The mailman had delivered that batch of letters tucked in the mailbox beside the dead skunk. Letters from the crabbiest lady in church—one of which held money to be delivered every week . . .

192

"I hope Old Lady Lutz likes the mailbox," I told Hummer. She nodded and smiled gently.

And now that I think of it, Hummer never did jab me or anyone else in the chest again.

WHAT'S UP THIS WEEK?
- Love Looks for the Best
- Love Is Not Self-Righteous
- Loving the Unlovable

PRAYER POWER
Love is such an important topic that it's worth spending another week learning more about it. We're going to dive in and find out more about what love looks like in real life. Sometimes it's tough to live in a loving way. Pray that God will help you grow in unselfish love, the kind of love he shows to us all the time.

LOVE LOOKS FOR THE BEST

We can all be critical at times. It's often easier to spot the faults in others than it is to appreciate the good. However, there is more to everyone than meets the eye. Love knows that and always looks for the best. Let's find out more about that.

BRAIN STRETCHERS

FOR KIDS:

1. In "Church Lady," what were Ricky's and Hummer's reasons for not liking Mrs. Lutz? Did they know her well enough to know what she was really like?

2. Do you ever forget to look for the best in others? How would you feel if someone chose not to like you without really getting to know you?

ASK AN ADULT:

1. Do you know anyone who is difficult to get along with? Is it hard for you to see his or her good qualities? How do you usually react to that person?

2. What good things have happened when you looked for the best in others?

SCRIPTURE POWER

Love never gives up, never loses faith, is always hopeful, and endures through every circumstance. (1 Corinthians 13:7)

This verse is from one of the most well-known Bible passages about love. The love it describes is one that has the highest goal in mind. It focuses on the best. It fights to keep believing. It is not a halfway deal.

Let love be your highest goal. (1 Corinthians 14:1)

Here again is the idea of the high goals of love. Love comes first, above everything else. When we feel like staying angry when someone hurts or angers us, we aren't choosing to make love our highest goal. Love forgives and moves on. It's not blind to hurts and pain. Instead, it deliberately chooses to continue to look for the best in others.

Love each other with genuine affection, and take delight in honoring each other. (Romans 12:10)

What does it mean to honor someone? Basically, it means to celebrate that person, paying attention to what's worthwhile and good in him or her. Genuine love delights in honoring others.

Whatever measure you use in judging others, it will be used to measure how you are judged. (Matthew 7:2)

Ricky and Hummer thought Mrs. Lutz was their enemy, or at least someone who wasn't very kind. However, their practical joke was not honoring to her. She appeared to them to be unloving, but she was more loving than they were. They judged her and then turned around and treated her very poorly instead of trying to see the good in her.

PRAYER POWER

Ask God today to open your eyes to all the good in the people you know. Sometimes it's tough to do; we all can be critical at times. But God will help you see others through his eyes when your heart is open.

LOVE IS NOT SELF-RIGHTEOUS

Self-righteousness means thinking of ourselves as better than others. Based on what we learned yesterday about love always looking for the best in others, it makes sense that there is no room for self-righteousness in love. We'll discuss more about it today.

BRAIN STRETCHERS

FOR KIDS:

1. What did you think of Ricky and Hummer's plans for a practical joke? Did you find it funny? Did you feel bad for Mrs. Lutz?
2. Was Mrs. Lutz really a bad person? What was wrong about the kids' attitude toward her?
3. Do you know anyone who always seems to think he or she is better than you? How does that make you feel?

ASK AN ADULT:

1. Has there ever been a time when you thought you were better than someone else? What made you realize that attitude was wrong? What did you do about it?

2. Has there ever been a time when someone didn't like you for no apparent reason? How did that make you feel?

SCRIPTURE POWER

Stop judging others, and you will not be judged. And why worry about a speck in your friend's eye when you have a log in your own? . . . First get rid of the log from your own eye; then perhaps you will see well enough to deal with the speck in your friend's eye. (Matthew 7:1, 3-5)

Self-righteousness is very similar to judging. Judging means finding fault in others; self-righteousness means thinking we're better than others. Neither sin shows love. Think about how Ricky's and Hummer's actions toward Mrs. Lutz would have been different if they hadn't judged her or been so self-righteous that they ignored their own wrong, self-righteous attitudes.

Love . . . keeps no record of when it has been wronged. (1 Corinthians 13:5)

Did Ricky and Hummer keep track of how they thought Mrs. Lutz had wronged them? Did Mrs. Lutz appear to keep track of how she had been hurt by the practical joke? She may not have known who did it, but it still must have hurt. In a loving way, she seemed to let it go and move on.

Now we see things imperfectly as in a poor mirror, but then we will see everything with perfect clarity. All that I know now is partial and incomplete, but then I will know everything completely, just as God knows me now. (1 Corinthians 13:12)

Ricky and Hummer did not have all the facts about Mrs. Lutz as a person before they assumed she was mean. Yes, they knew her a little from church, but they didn't know all the good things she was doing. They saw imperfectly, like the verse says. Self-righteous attitudes are very destructive. They keep us from seeing all the good in someone, and they limit our ability to see others as potential friends.

PRAYER POWER

Talk to God about possible attitudes of self-righteousness in yourself. We often can't see those attitudes in ourselves, but the Holy Spirit will reveal them to us when we sincerely want him to show us.

LOVING THE UNLOVABLE

Sometimes we meet people who seem irritable, cranky, selfish, or mean—all in all, completely unlovable. What should our response be to them? You guessed it—we should act with love.

BRAIN STRETCHERS
FOR KIDS:

1. What are some qualities that make someone difficult to love? Do you have any of those qualities?
2. Do you know anyone at school or in church who seems unlovable? Can you think of any ways to share God's love with that person?

ASK AN ADULT:

1. Is there anyone who is unlovable to God (besides the devil)?
2. What are some good ways you can act toward someone who seems difficult to love?

SCRIPTURE POWER

Most important of all, continue to show deep love for each other, for love covers a multitude of sins.
(1 Peter 4:8)

Check out the first four words of that verse: *Most important of all.* That means this task is number one. Now look at the next word: *continue.* That means don't stop. These five words tell us something about the importance of showing deep love for others. Just as Jesus' love covers our sins, our love for others should be greater than their sins. That goes for people who seem easy to love as well as for those who aren't so nice.

Be patient with each other, making allowance for each other's faults because of your love. (Ephesians 4:2)

No one is perfect, and we all need to learn patience. Love allows others to make mistakes and to have faults. Love doesn't depend on the goodness of the other person. God's love doesn't depend on our goodness. We can't earn it, but he loves us anyway—completely and forever. That's a high example to follow!

Love your enemies! Pray for those who persecute you! In that way, you will be acting as true children of your Father in heaven. . . . If you love only those who love you, what good is that? Even corrupt tax collectors do that much. If you are kind only to your friends, how are you different from anyone else? Even pagans do that. (Matthew 5:44-47)

If your enemies are hungry, feed them. If they are thirsty, give them something to drink. (Romans 12:20)

Friends are easy to love, right? How much harder it is to love people who hate us! But since love doesn't depend on the other person's goodness, we are free to love our enemies. Pretty interesting, huh? Love has a way of changing people.

Who knows which of your enemies could become friends with a little love?

> *Do for others what you would like them to do for you.* *(Matthew 7:12)*

You might know that verse as the Golden Rule. Would you like to be treated the way you treat others? That's a good question to keep in mind.

PRAYER POWER

What is your level of love for "unlovable" people? Do you need God to do a heart adjustment in you? Talk to him about it. Thank him for his perfect example of love, and ask him to grow his love in you so you'll want to share it with other people—even the difficult ones.

CONCLUDING THOUGHTS

They say you shouldn't judge a book by its cover. When you judge a book by its cover, you might miss a really great story by passing over a book that doesn't have a really cool-looking cover on it.

In "Church Lady," Ricky and Hummer decided to play a Halloween prank on Mrs. Lutz because they thought she was a mean Sunday school teacher. She seemed so crabby that it made Ricky dislike going to Sunday school at all. So why shouldn't they have done something mean to her? She deserved it, didn't she?

They judged Mrs. Lutz, although they didn't know her well enough to know the good in her heart. They decided to do something mean to her based on the little contact they'd had with her. Their attitudes toward Mrs. Lutz changed when they found out more about her character—that she was a very giving person. In fact, her thoughtfulness had been a blessing to Hummer over and over again. They learned something about looking for the best in others and about not being self-righteous.

How are you doing with showing love to others, even the unlovable ones?

LINE IT UP!

It's time for some love in action! Think of someone in your life you don't know very well but who either seems difficult to like or who seems to need a friend. Maybe that person is an acquaintance at school or at church. Make a point in the next week or so to say or do something kind to that person. If he or she responds well, then great. If not, then pray that God will help that person feel loved by him. Maybe he'll use you to do that. Will you be open to it?

PRAYER POWER

We've just finished two weeks of studying what love is. What are your thoughts now? Share them with God. He loves you more than you could ever understand. Pretty amazing, right?

WEEK 11

WHAT'S UP THIS WEEK:
The Adventure of Faith

THEME VERSE FOR THE WEEK:
Hebrews 10:38

A righteous person will live by faith.

In "Things Unseen," Tyce Sanders faces a life-threatening situation on the planet Mars. Will the experience help him to understand what real faith is?

Editor's Note: Catch more of Tyce's adventures in Sigmund Brouwer's exciting Mars Diaries series, published by Tyndale House Publishers.

Things Unseen

With time running out, Mom wants me, Tyce Sanders, to write this into a report for a magazine on Earth. She thinks it will mean more to people coming from a guy my age than from any scientist. But I hardly know where to begin. I mean, everything is happening at once. First my argument with Mom about church stuff. Then how it seems my body is getting too weak to move my wheelchair. And how Mom—a scientist herself—has just reported that the oxygen level in the colony is dropping so fast that all of us barely have a month to live.

Let me say this first to anyone on Earth who might read this when we are gone: If you have legs that don't work, Mars is probably a better place to be than Earth. That's only a guess, of course, because I am the only person in the entire history of humankind who has never breathed Earth air or felt Earth gravity.

I'm not kidding.

You see, I'm the only person ever born on Mars. Everyone else here came from Earth about 6 ½ years ago—12 Earth years to you—as part of the first expedition to set up a colony. The trip took eight months, and during this voyage my mother and father fell in love with each other. Mom is a scientist. Dad is a space pilot. They were the first couple to be married on Mars—and the last, for now. They loved each other so much that they married by exchanging their vows over radiophone with a preacher on Earth. When I was born half a Mars year later, it made things so complicated on the colony that it was decided there would be no more marriages and babies until the colony was better established.

Complicated?

Let me put it this way. Because of planetary orbits, spaceships can only reach Mars every three years. (Only three ships have arrived since I was born.) And with what it costs to send a ship from Earth, cargo space is expensive—very, very expensive. Diapers, baby bottles, cribs, and carriages are not exactly a priority for interplanetary travel. I did without all that stuff. Just like I did without a modern hospital when I was born. So when my legs came out funny, there was no one to fix them. Which is why I'm in a wheelchair.

It could be worse, of course. On Earth, I'd weigh 90 pounds. Here, I'm only 34 pounds. That makes it easier to get around—at least when my body and arms aren't weak from lack of oxygen.

The other good thing is that I never have to travel far. On Earth you can go in one direction for thousands of miles.

Here, all 50 of us—mainly scientists and workers—live under a sealed dome that might cover four of your football fields. (I know all of this about Earth because of the CD-books I scan for hours every day.)

When I'm not being taught by my computer, I spend my time wheeling around the paths beneath the colony dome. I know every scientist and worker by first name. I know every path past every minidome, the small, dark, plastic huts where people live in privacy from the others. I've seen every color of Martian sky through the superclear plastic of the main dome above us. I've spent hours listening to sandstorms rattle over us. I've . . .

. . . I've got to go. Mom's calling for me to join her for mealtime.

▼ ▼ ▼ ▼ ▼

Our minidome, like everyone else's, had two office-bedrooms and a common living space. Mom was waiting for me in one of the chairs outside my room.

I grunted as I pushed the wheelchair. It was getting harder and harder to move it. I worried that pretty soon I might not be able to move it at all.

I finally reached her. She handed me a plastic nutrient tube. Red.

"Spaghetti and meatballs?" I asked.

She nodded. (I've never tasted real spaghetti and meatballs, of course, so I have to take Mom's word for it that the nute-tube stuff is not nearly as good as the real thing.)

As usual, she prayed over it.

As usual, I didn't.

As usual, it made her sad.

209

"Our oxygen level is dropping faster and faster," she said.

"How can I convince you to consider faith in God? If we only have a month left . . . "

"I only believe what I can see or measure," I said. In the colony, I'm surrounded by scientists. All their experiments are on data that can be measured.

"But faith is the hope in things unseen," she said. "Otherwise it wouldn't be a matter of faith. We don't see your Dad, but we know he loves us, no matter where his cargo ship is. Faith in God is like that."

"Mom . . . " We had argued about this a lot.

Mom knew she could never force me to believe something if I didn't want to. No person can make another person believe. They can only make another person *pretend* to believe. But Mom preferred to keep our discussion going by letting me express my doubts. Faith, she said, grew stronger through doubt.

I ripped off the top of my nute-tube. Most of the scientists needed to use a knife. I didn't. My arms and hands were much stronger than theirs because I had been in the wheelchair as long as I could remember.

I guzzled the red paste. "I'm going," I said. Mom and I were good friends, but we were both grumpy from a big argument we'd had recently and the oxygen problem. I needed time by myself.

She didn't ask me where I was going. She didn't need to. There isn't much room in the dome for me to get lost.

By the time I wheeled to the center of the dome 15 minutes later, I was sweating from the effort. Before, it only would have taken a couple of minutes and hardly any muscle power. This oxygen thing was scary. But what could I do about it?

Around me, men and women scientists walked on the

paths, going from minidome to minidome for whatever business they had. They nodded or said hello as they walked around me.

In my wheelchair, I nodded and said hello back. Other than that, I just stared upward at the purples and oranges of the clouds above the dome. Other people on other expeditions might one day explore the planet outside. Not us. We would be dead soon. Dad was piloting the next cargo ship, and it wouldn't arrive for two months—one month after the colony dome ran out of oxygen.

I kept staring upward. My eyes drifted to the giant, dark solar panels that hung just below the clear roof of the dome. These were the solar panels that were killing us. They turned the energy of sunlight into electricity. Part of this electricity powered our computers and other equipment. Most of the electricity, though, went as a current into the water of the oxygen tank. The electrical current broke the water—H_2O—into the gases of hydrogen and oxygen, two parts hydrogen for every one part of oxygen. The hydrogen was used as fuel for some of the generators. The oxygen, of course, we breathed.

But something was wrong with the panels. Nobody could figure it out. Taken down and tested, they worked perfectly. But back up at the roof, the panels were making less and less electricity each day. With less power, we had less oxygen. It was that simple.

As I stared at the panels, wondering about the problem, I heard huffing and puffing. I turned my shoulders to see bald-headed George, a computer tech, pushing a cart toward me.

He caught my glance. "Either these carts are getting heavier," he said, wiping his brow, "or there's even less oxygen in the dome than we figure."

He pushed on.

Everybody is losing strength, I thought, *not just me.*

I fought a burp as I felt my stomach rumble from the spaghetti-and-meatball paste from lunch.

Hang on, I thought as I remembered lunch. If I was getting weaker, how come I'd been able to rip open my nute-tube like always?

I thought about it some more. What if it wasn't me getting weaker but my wheelchair slowly getting harder to push? And what if George wasn't losing oxygen but the cart was getting harder to push?

Weird, I told myself. Why would things with wheels be getting harder to push? And how could it be happening so gradually that we didn't notice?

I heard a squeak high above me. I looked up. I heard one more squeak. *From the solar panels?*

I glanced at my watch. Then I had a wild idea.

"Mom!" I shouted. "Mom!"

As fast as I could, I wheeled back toward our minidome.

▼ ▼ ▼ ▼ ▼

Two hours later, Mom came back from her laboratory. I was sitting on the bed, because my wheelchair was still at the lab.

"Well?" I asked.

"Things unseen," she said, smiling. "Microscopic particles of Martian sand that had gotten into the sealed dome over the years. We took apart your wheelchair axle and examined the grease that helps it turn. The sand has finally worn it down."

"Wheelchair wheels," I said. "Wheels on a cart. And the tiny wheels that let the solar panels follow the sun! The more sand, the harder it is for all the wheels to turn."

"Exactly," she said. "That was the squeak you heard. We were looking for the problem in the panels and all along it was something as simple as the wheels. Technicians have already fixed the problem!"

She high-fived me. I hardly noticed, I was thinking so hard.

"Things unseen," I said. "Isn't that what you just said? Things that are there but you don't know it until you know where to look or how?" I grinned at her, finally understanding. "Like we don't know enough about what's behind faith but someday we'll find out?"

She high-fived me again. It was answer enough.

WHAT'S UP THIS WEEK?
- Faith Defined
- Faith Is a Risk
- Faith Is Life-Changing

PRAYER POWER
What do you know about faith? No matter if we know a little or a lot about it, God always has more to show us. Ask him to reveal new truths to you about believing in him.

FAITH DEFINED

Faith is like trust. It's counting on someone or something to be true and reliable, even without being able to see all the outcomes. Let's take a look:

BRAIN STRETCHERS
FOR KIDS:

1. In "Things Unseen," what is the definition Tyce's mom gives him of faith? Tyce says he believes only things he can ____ or ____. Do you remember what those two things are?
2. What do you think is wrong with Tyce's viewpoint?

ASK AN ADULT:

1. Tyce's mom told him that faith grows stronger through doubt. Has that ever happened to you or to anyone you know?
2. What are some things you could say about your faith to people who don't believe in God?

SCRIPTURE POWER

What is faith? It is the confident assurance that what we hope for is going to happen. It is the evidence of things we cannot yet see. (Hebrews 11:1)

There you have it. The evidence of things we cannot see. Isn't that what Tyce's mom said? Smart woman. She must have read her Bible. We aren't supposed to have all the answers to have faith. Faith requires a little blind guts. However, the value of our faith is entirely dependent on the strength and trustworthiness of whomever we put our faith in. Confusing? Maybe this will clarify: Which would you rather trust to hold a mug of hot chocolate over your lap: a wet paper towel or a sturdy piece of wood? A commercial for a paper towel might claim that it could hold the mug, but tests would show otherwise. But wood would be a tried and true choice. God has shown and continues to prove his faithfulness. He will never let you down.

By faith we understand that the entire universe was formed at God's command, that what we now see did not come from anything that can be seen. (Hebrews 11:3)

This is an appropriate verse for a story set on Mars. If you've ever looked at the night sky and wondered how many stars are up there, maybe you feel some awe at just how big it all is. God created the whole universe, and he still runs the entire show with amazing precision. Since he handles all that so perfectly, he certainly can handle the details of our life.

Your faith is far more precious to God than mere gold. So if your faith remains strong after being tried by fiery trials, it will bring you much praise and glory and honor on the day when Jesus Christ is revealed to the whole world. (1 Peter 1:7)

215

Faith is tough. Gutsy. And it's precious to God. When our faith is tested and it remains strong, God is pleased.

> What's the use of saying you have faith if you don't prove it by your actions? That kind of faith can't save anyone. . . . Faith that doesn't show itself by good deeds is no faith at all—it is dead and useless. (James 2:14-17)

Faith, like love, requires action! Our genuine faith in God will result in a desire to do good. Faith and deeds can't be separated. They are a package deal—one builds on the other.

> You love him even though you have never seen him. Though you do not see him, you trust him; and even now you are happy with a glorious, inexpressible joy. Your reward for trusting him will be the salvation of your souls. (1 Peter 1:8-9)

We cannot receive eternal salvation without putting our faith in Jesus Christ, who died and rose again. This takes risk, which we'll discuss more tomorrow.

PRAYER POWER

What have you learned about faith so far? It's a big concept, but knowing God's character more every day helps us understand his idea of faith. Ask him to help you see what he requires of you concerning faith.

FAITH IS A RISK

Ready for adventure in your life? If you're a person of faith in God, then you can count on some thrills and spills over the years. Faith is a risk. Let's find out more about that today.

BRAIN STRETCHERS

FOR KIDS:

1. What risks did Tyce face living on Mars? Would you have felt scared in his place?
2. Is it ever difficult for you to trust God?

ASK AN ADULT:

1. Can you think of a time when you wished you had more information but you had to trust God? How did that make you feel?
2. What have you learned about God that helps you have faith in him?

SCRIPTURE POWER

Don't you remember that our ancestor Abraham was declared right with God because of what he did when he offered his son Isaac on the altar? You see, he was trusting God so much that he was willing to do whatever God told him to do. His faith was made complete by what he did— by his actions. (James 2:21-22)

By its very nature, faith involves risk. To some people who have to have all the scientific facts, faith may seem ignorant. To those of us who know God, faith is the biggest adventure of life! Abraham may have wondered how God could ask him to sacrifice Isaac. But his faith in God was so great that he trusted God with the outcome. Abraham's faith helped him trust God's character to be consistent.

One day near Horesh, David received the news that Saul was on the way to Ziph to search for him and kill him. Jonathan went to find David and encouraged him to stay strong in his faith in God. (1 Samuel 23:15-16)

The risk of faith requires strength and an adventurous spirit. King David showed this spirit and his faith in God from the time he was young. God may be asking you to step out and take a risk of faith. Maybe there's someone with whom he wants you to share the good news of salvation. Maybe there's a bold stand he wants you to take for something you know is right. Maybe he wants you to say no to giving in to negative peer pressure.

In every battle you will need faith as your shield to stop the fiery arrows aimed at you by Satan. (Ephesians 6:16)

Faith is essential for battling the temptations Satan throws our way. He hates our faith in God, so of course he's going to attack it. Our faith needs to stay strong and active, grounded in a growing relationship with God.

PRAYER POWER

Does the idea of adventure send a thrill through you? Living for God is the greatest adventure you could ever hope to experience. Ask him today to help you each day and guide you as you put your faith in him. He has awesome plans for you. Take the risk and believe him!

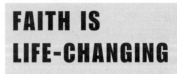

FAITH IS LIFE-CHANGING

Real faith changes people. It makes the impossible possible. Here are a few thoughts:

BRAIN STRETCHERS
FOR KIDS:

1. How did Tyce's frightening experience with the oxygen shortage change his views about faith in God?
2. Is faith exciting to you, or is it scary sometimes? If so, when is it scary?

ASK AN ADULT:

1. Has your life been changed because of your faith in God? In what ways?
2. How is life better for you than for people who don't have faith in God?

SCRIPTURE POWER

Jesus told them, "I assure you, if you have faith and don't doubt, you can do things like this and much more. You can even say to this mountain, 'May God lift you up and throw you

*into the sea,' and it will happen. If you believe, you
will receive whatever you ask for in prayer." (Matthew
21:21-22)*

Look at what Jesus said about the unbelievable power of
faith. This is big-time stuff! How will your life be changed
because of your faith?

*Jesus responded, "Didn't I tell you that you will see God's
glory if you believe?" (John 11:40)*

Our belief, or faith, in God opens the door for him to work.
He loves to show his glory, and he wants to do it in your life.
That puts you in a very special role. Each of us has the opportunity to partner with God to do his work in the world. That
is the way to abundant life, and it's a surefire way to see
God's glory over and over again. That is one opportunity not
to be missed!

*It was by faith that Abel brought a more acceptable offer-
ing to God than Cain did. . . . It was by faith that Enoch
was taken up to heaven without dying. . . . It was by faith
that Noah built an ark to save his family from the flood.
. . . It was by faith that Abraham obeyed when God called
him to leave home and go to another land that God
would give to him as his inheritance. He went without
knowing where he was going. . . . It was by faith that
Sarah together with Abraham was able to have a child,
even though they were too old and Sarah was barren.
Abraham believed that God would keep his promise.
(Hebrews 11:4-11)*

We have the benefit of a rich heritage of believers in God.
God has changed many people's lives, and he wants to do

just such amazing things in our life. We just need to put our faith in him.

> *Therefore, since we are surrounded by such a huge crowd of witnesses to the life of faith, let us strip off every weight that slows us down, especially the sin that so easily hinders our progress. And let us run with endurance the race that God has set before us. We do this by keeping our eyes on Jesus, on whom our faith depends from start to finish. (Hebrews 12:1-2)*

Finally, where should our focus be? We need to plant our eyes firmly on Jesus. He is the ultimate example of faith, because his death on the cross proved God's faithfulness and love more than any other event in the history of the universe. When we let go of our sinful habits and make God our first priority in life, there is no limit to how he can work in and through us. Are you ready for the adventure?

PRAYER POWER

What do you think of this week's study on faith? Spend a little extra time in prayer today, asking God to show you the state of your faith right now. He'll show you areas where you need to grow, sins you need to get rid of, and just how much he loves your faith in him.

CONCLUDING THOUGHTS

Tyce struggled with believing. Actually, he downright fought the whole idea of faith. Just like God showed Tyce a thing or two about faith, God will reveal himself to anyone whose heart is open to listen and learn. God can even prepare a person to become more open to faith.

It took a pretty harrowing experience to turn Tyce's heart to God. You may know people who don't want to have anything to do with God. They may even mock your beliefs. Don't give up on them! God never gives up, and he wants us to keep praying for the people he puts in our lives.

Be bold. Be strong. There's a task ahead of you that will require greater faith. Prepare now to be ready for it. Spending time reading God's Word, praying, and hanging out with friends who encourage you to grow in your relationship with God will help get you ready to answer God's call to the adventure of faith.

Get ready!

LINE IT UP!

Do you have an idea yet about what God might call you to do for him? Are you willing to say yes to whatever he asks, taking a step of faith to trust him with everything? Spend some time with your family or Bible study friends, simply discussing your faith and God's possible calling on your life. Sometimes it helps to gain insight from other people who are running the same race of faith. You may get some serious wisdom from the talk.

PRAYER POWER

Once you've had the "Line It Up!" discussion, spend some time talking to God about insights you may have gained from your discussions. Ask him to keep working on you to hear what he's telling you about faith. God bless your adventure! It's going to be a great one!

WHAT'S UP THIS WEEK:
How Honest Is Honest?

THEME VERSE FOR THE WEEK:
Psalm 32:2

Yes, what joy for those whose record the Lord
has cleared of sin, whose lives are lived in complete honesty!

What exactly is a lie? What if no one gets hurt? This week George learns a lesson about what honesty really is.

Golden Tonsils

On the second day of summer vacation at my uncle's farm, I forgot to shut the wooden peg on the chicken-coop door. By the time I remembered, the only chickens still inside were old or fat. The other dozen had vanished into the bramble bushes at the south end of the farmyard.

I wasn't worried, though—call me a creative genius.

Well, first call me George. That's my name. Then call me a creative genius. Or maybe call me the boy with the golden tonsils.

Why?

City slicker or not, I can talk my way out of any trouble, smooth enough that you'd think my throat and tonsils were made of gold. Jealous people with less imagination will insist that my stories are lies, but I know lies are different. Lies are false statements that hurt other people. My stories are more like a rearrangement of the truth, and if people draw the wrong conclusions, that's their problem.

At this moment, of course, my problem was the lack of chickens inside the chicken coop. How could a kid from the city know chickens move so fast?

"Geooorrgge!"

I scrambled backwards from where I'd been crawling into the bushes.

My aunt—a huge woman, dressed as usual in jeans and a plaid shirt—stood beside the chicken coop. Which explained her less-than-happy tone.

"Geooorrgge!"

I tried standing too soon and snagged my arm on a dead branch. Ouch.

"Geooorr—" Aunt Stella stopped her bellow as soon as she saw me. "Get your skinny neck here where I can wring it!"

Behind my back, I dropped the feed grain that I had thought would be good bait to tempt the chickens back into the coop. I walked slowly to give myself time for my creative genius to kick in. That's when I noticed the blood trickling down my forearm from where I had snagged it.

A glimmer of an idea hit.

"George," my aunt said as I got near. "Half of my chickens are gone. The other half are upset and squawking. They won't lay eggs all week. A body might think some boy had been terrorizing them."

Not terrorizing. Just lifting them to count eggs. Somehow it didn't seem like the right time to mention my interest in farm arithmetic. So I let my golden tonsils take care of the problem.

"Could a big stray dog be smart enough to push up the wooden peg with its nose?" I asked. "And then run away as I was walking by?"

Had I told a lie? No sir. I'd merely asked a couple of questions.

She dropped her hands from her hips. "A stray dog! After my prize hens?"

I shrugged. Amazing what conclusions people can draw. And who could get hurt from this?

"Where'd it go?" she asked. "Did you get a good look at it?"

I held out my arm for her inspection, meaning for her to decide from my cut that I'd chased the dog into the bushes.

My aunt's eyes widened as she saw the cut on my arm and the blood. "It snapped at you?"

Those conclusions were better than I could have hoped for.

"I was in the bushes," I said. "Where the chickens went." Both statements were true, weren't they?

Aunt Stella spun on her heels.

"Quick," she said. "Into the house."

Inside, with calm efficiency, she led me to the kitchen sink, ran cold water over my arm, then dabbed on disinfectant.

"It's one thing to chase chickens," she said. "But it's another to attack a boy."

I kept my mouth shut as she applied a Band-Aid. Her face had a thoughtful expression.

"Could be this dog has rabies," she said in a suddenly serious tone. "A dog's got to be out of its mind to attack a human for no reason."

"Rabies?"

"Yup. Was the dog frothing at the mouth?"

"I didn't see," I said. More truth, right?

"Don't matter. You'll still need a rabies shot."

"Rabies shot?"

229

"A needle injection into the marrow of your hip bone. Much as it will hurt, we can't take any chances. Rabies is contagious and deadly."

"Rabies shot?"

She patted my head. "First, we get the dog."

Then she whirled away and reached the telephone before I could think of a reply. She dialed, held the receiver to her ear, waited a few seconds, then spoke quickly. "Fred? It's Stella. Can you round up a few of your boys and get here as quick as you can? I'll explain when you arrive. And Fred . . . bring rifles."

Rifles?

Aunt Stella hung up the phone. "Your uncle said he'd be in town all day, and we can't afford to let that dog get away."

"Aunt Stella . . . "

She waved away my protest. "You're going upstairs to lie quietly in a darkened room. If you don't get worked up, I suspect we can delay our hospital visit until that dog is shot."

Shot?

She led me upstairs to my bedroom and pulled down the shades.

"Remember," she said. "Don't move. I'm going to make a few more calls and we'll have enough help to round up every dog in the county."

I heard the murmur of her voice downstairs, then everything was quiet as the screen door slammed behind her. Minutes later, the roar of pickup trucks pulling into the yard reached me. I tiptoed to the shades, pulled them back, and looked down.

Four men stepped from two trucks. All with rifles.

I groaned and staggered back to the bed.

How could my creative genius get me out of this? Especially when I wasn't allowed to leave the room.

Then I relaxed at a new thought. How could they find a dog that didn't exist?

Then I tensed at a newer thought. A needle jabbed right into my hip bone?

I stared at the ceiling, alone with my worries and the ticking of the alarm clock. Fifteen minutes had passed when my Aunt Stella yelled up to my bedroom.

"Georrrggeee! Take a peek outside!"

I did. She and the four men below had a huge black dog, feet roped and bound, lying on its side in the dust. Where had they found it?

"Is this it?" she shouted.

I thought for a moment. Must be just a stray dog. They'd take it to the vet and check it for the rabies it certainly didn't have. Then they'd let it go. No rabies, and I wouldn't need a rabies shot, and that dog would never tell a soul that it hadn't been chasing chickens.

Perfect.

"Is this it?" she repeated.

"It sure looks mean." Creative nonlying at its best.

She nodded with satisfaction, then she said something I couldn't hear to the men. The four men lifted the dog onto a blanket and carried it toward the barn.

What could this mean?

I dashed downstairs, bolted through the kitchen, and skidded to a stop outside in front of Aunt Stella. The men had already disappeared.

"Aren't they taking the dog to the vet?" I gasped.

She shook her head. "Rabies is too serious to take

chances. They'll shoot it first, then they'll take some blood in for testing."

My mouth must have dropped.

"Something wrong, George?"

"Yes," I said. And I began running. "Don't shoot! Don't shoot!"

I got halfway to the barn before it happened. Two shots boomed, one after the other. Then silence.

I fell to my knees in stunned horror. I didn't realize I was on the ground and crying until Aunt Stella placed a hand on my shoulder.

"Something wrong, George?"

"They killed an innocent dog," I sobbed. "Innocent!"

"But George, you said . . . "

"I let you think it," I said as I wiped my face. "I never dreamed . . . "

I told her the truth. All of it.

She helped me to my feet.

"Fred," she called to the barn. "Come on out for that coffee and pie I promised you and the boys."

As I rubbed my eyes, the four men walked into the sunlight. Followed by the huge black dog.

"It's . . . it's not dead?"

"'Course not, George. You think a country girl like me couldn't tell the difference between a scratch and a dog bite? Soon as I started laying that Band-Aid on your arm, I got an idea."

"You mean . . . ?"

"I mean as soon as I got you upstairs, I called Fred back to let him in on my little joke. And I asked him to hide his dog in a blanket. Soon as you weren't looking, we pulled the dog out and roped it good. I kept waiting to see when you'd finally start telling the truth. I thanked the Lord that you busted so hard getting down from your bedroom."

I smiled weakly.

"The way I figure it, George," she continued, "remembering those two shots should keep you honest for a long while."

She paused. "That, and about five hours of shoveling out pig stalls to pay for the missing chickens."

Fred and his grown boys and the dog were almost up to us by now. I was suddenly conscious of my tear-streaked face.

"Dust in my eyes from falling," I started to tell them automatically. "Made my eyes water like this . . . "

I remembered those two shots from the barn.

"Actually, I was crying like a baby," I said quickly. "Um, mind if I pet your dog?"

WHAT'S UP THIS WEEK?
- Creative Nonlying
- No One Gets Hurt?
- Freedom in Honesty

PRAYER POWER
How much do you really want to be honest about honesty? There's a question! Do you think God sees room for improvement in your honesty level? Ask him what he thinks, and open your mind and heart to agree with his Word about living in complete honesty.

CREATIVE NONLYING

Huh? George used that term in the story to describe what he does when he doesn't actually tell a lie with his mouth but he allows someone to believe something that's not true. God has some things to say about that.

BRAIN STRETCHERS
FOR KIDS:

1. How does George define lying at the beginning of "Golden Tonsils"? What does he say to explain how his stories are different from lying?
2. How did George lie without saying anything at all?

ASK AN ADULT:

1. What do you think are some reasons people lie?
2. Has there ever been a time when you let someone believe something that wasn't true? What happened? Would you do it again?

SCRIPTURE POWER

My people bend their tongues like bows to shoot lies. They refuse to stand up for the truth. And they only go from bad to worse! (Jeremiah 9:3)

Notice the phrase *bend their tongues*? If you've ever heard the similiar phrase *bend the truth,* then maybe you'll understand that a lie doesn't have to be completely the opposite of the truth to be a lie. Letting someone believe something that isn't true is being less than honest. Someone who lives in complete honesty will "stand up for the truth," as the verse goes on to say. Honesty requires decisive boldness. It's a conscious decision to keep from bending the truth at all.

> *"They all take advantage of one another and spread their slanderous lies. They all fool and defraud each other; no one tells the truth. With practiced tongues they tell lies; they wear themselves out with all their sinning. They pile lie upon lie and utterly refuse to come to me," says the Lord. (Jeremiah 9:4-6)*

Take advantage is another phrase that broadens the definition of a lie. A lie happens anytime someone is taken advantage of or deceived into believing something untrue.

> *Those who use trickery to pervert justice and tell lies to tear down the innocent will be no more. (Isaiah 29:21)*

Trickery. There is yet another term that falls into the "lying" category. Of course, some tricks are played in complete fun. But when trickery is used to bend the truth or to take advantage of someone, it's a lie. George certainly bent the truth and took advantage of what he thought Aunt Stella would believe when he didn't confess to knowing how the chickens escaped. He knew the truth, but he chose not to reveal it in

235

order to avoid getting in trouble. In the end, his lie came back to haunt him and he wound up in trouble anyway.

A false witness will not go unpunished, nor will a liar escape. (Proverbs 19:5)

A false witness is someone who knows the truth but doesn't stand up for it, leading others to believe a lie to be true. George was a false witness because he *did* witness exactly how the chickens escaped, but he didn't speak up for the truth. The truth always wins in the end, and George did not escape the consequences of being a false witness.

But you desire honesty from the heart, so you can teach me to be wise in my inmost being. (Psalm 51:6)

A person who is wise in his inmost being will show honesty even in the little things. No room for creative nonlies!

PRAYER POWER

Pray and ask God to reveal to you the times you may be tempted to lie with a creative nonlie. Ask him to develop more honesty in your heart.

NO ONE GETS HURT?

George was clueless as to how his creative nonlying techniques were causing hurt. By the end of the story, he got a clue that someone *always* gets hurt by a lie.

BRAIN STRETCHERS

FOR KIDS:

1. How does it seem Aunt Stella feels about George's lie in "Golden Tonsils"? Does she agree with his idea of a creative nonlie?
2. Can you be close friends with someone if you lie to each other? Why or why not?
3. What happens to your trust in someone if that person has lied to you?

ASK AN ADULT:

1. Why is lying bad, even if no one knows you're lying?
2. Have you ever been hurt because someone lied to you?

SCRIPTURE POWER

The Lord hates cheating, but he delights in honesty. Good people are guided by their honesty; treacherous people are destroyed by their dishonesty. The godly are directed by their honesty; the wicked fall beneath their load of sin. (Proverbs 11:1, 3, 5)

Honesty guides good people, while dishonesty brings destruction. To whom? Well, to the liars themselves. Didn't George's lie bring trouble to him? He wound up earning a healthy dose of discipline in the form of five hours of shoveling out pig stalls. Lying also causes God pain because it is sinning. God hurts every time we sin. Anytime we aren't completely honest, or we allow someone to believe something contrary to what we know is true, we are hurting God. So even if it seems like no one gets hurt, God does.

If a ruler honors liars, all his advisers will be wicked. (Proverbs 29:12)

Imagine a nation whose leaders are corrupt. The effects of their dishonesty touch everyone living in that country, as well as other nations who deal with those leaders.

"I will put you on trial. I will be a ready witness against all sorcerers and adulterers and liars. I will speak against those who cheat employees of their wages, who oppress widows and orphans, or who deprive the foreigners living among you of justice, for these people do not fear me," says the Lord Almighty. (Malachi 3:5)

God takes lying seriously. So seriously, in fact, that he lumps liars in the same category as sorcerers and adulterers and describes the destructive effects of such sin.

Here is a description of worthless and wicked people: They are constant liars. . . . Their perverted hearts plot evil. They stir up trouble constantly. But they will be destroyed suddenly, broken beyond all hope of healing. (Proverbs 6:12-15)

Liars stir up trouble, hurting others as well as facing self-destruction. No good comes from lying. Its effects can be far-reaching, destroying trust that may never be regained. Lying causes pain. That's good for all of us to remember.

PRAYER POWER

What are your thoughts today about your own level of honesty? Tell God. Have you heard him speaking to you on this topic? Tell him what you think he's saying to you. Then respond with an open mind and heart in surrender to living in complete honesty.

FREEDOM IN HONESTY

If lying causes pain, then honesty certainly brings healing and freedom. Imagine a guilt-free life, knowing that there is nothing to fear from being caught in a lie. Here's more on the freedom of honesty:

BRAIN STRETCHERS
FOR KIDS:

1. In "Golden Tonsils," why does George think lying will make his life easier? Does it really make life easier, or does it trap him?
2. Have you ever been caught lying? What were the consequences?

ASK AN ADULT:

1. Have you ever felt guilty because you told a lie? Did you end up telling the truth later?
2. What do you think "freedom in honesty" means?

SCRIPTURE POWER

Because of the sinful things they say, because of the evil that is on their lips, let them be captured by their pride, their curses, and their lies. (Psalm 59:12)

Liars are eventually captured by their sin. Sin has a way of binding us in its grip, squeezing out the freedom Jesus wants to give us.

Finally, I confessed all my sins to you and stopped trying to hide them. I said to myself, "I will confess my rebellion to the Lord." And you forgave me! All my guilt is gone. (Psalm 32:5)

Confession brings freedom! No more guilt; only forgiveness from God and a chance to do things right the next time. An honest person has nothing to hide. Hiding the truth takes energy, and sin eventually tires out a person.

As long as I live, while I have breath from God, my lips will speak no evil, and my tongue will speak no lies. . . . I will maintain my innocence without wavering. My conscience is clear for as long as I live. (Job 27:3-4, 6)

Imagine living with a clear conscience. That is energizing. Think about how dragged down you feel when you know you've done something wrong. It's awful, isn't it? Lying is a sure way to wear ourselves out. It's a downward spiral. But a person who lives with a clear conscience, free of guilt, will live with the freedom of being innocent. It's a wonderful way to live!

If you want a happy life and good days, keep your tongue from speaking evil, and keep your lips from telling lies. (1 Peter 3:10)

That's a great last word on the awesome blessings of living free of lies. What more can be said?

241

PRAYER POWER

Talk to God today about your desire to live in the freedom of an honest life. Ask him to show you more and more how obeying his commands brings blessing.

CONCLUDING THOUGHTS

There's no such thing as a white lie—they're all dark.

A white lie is supposedly a small one that doesn't really hurt anybody. It's just a little variation from the truth that will help us avoid a nasty situation and make our life a little easier. If no one is going to get hurt from it, it can't be all that bad, right? We usually have to convince ourselves that a little lie is no big deal, because our conscience often tells us something different.

In "Golden Tonsils," George was the master of the white lie. He knew that he could talk his way out of just about anything. He had practiced his skill and had many successes in the past. After the chickens got out, he knew he'd have to be especially creative to get out of trouble. Things seemed to work out quite well when a mysterious dog got the blame for the missing chickens.

Telling a small lie leads us to tell bigger ones. With each lie, it gets a little easier to tell the next one. Before we know it, we are lying all the time. It

almost becomes second nature. We fool ourselves into thinking it's okay and that it isn't hurting anyone. We often hurt others when we are dishonest, and we hurt ourselves. We also hurt God, who sees our heart.

George learned the importance of telling the truth. His dishonesty led him into a nearly disastrous situation in which a dog could have been killed, and he almost got a painful and unnecessary rabies shot. George came to his senses and told the truth. Telling the truth can be tough sometimes, but the end result is always better.

LINE IT UP!

Is there any lie you've told, or a creative nonlie you've allowed someone to believe? This week's "Line It Up!" could be the most challenging one yet, but it is a necessary one to get us back into a right relationship with God and with someone who deserves the truth. Go ahead and have the guts to speak honestly. Confess the lie to whoever needs to hear the truth, including God. Then enjoy the freedom that comes from knowing God has forgiven you and there's only honesty between you and him now.

PRAYER POWER

Spend some time talking to God about honesty in every area of life, even the little things. Ask him to keep your heart honest. He'll give you the strength you need to stand up for the truth.

WEEK 13

WHAT'S UP THIS WEEK:
Being an Encourager

THEME VERSES FOR THE WEEK:
1 Thessalonians 5:11, 14

So encourage each other and build each other up, just as you are already doing. . . . Brothers and sisters, we urge you to warn those who are lazy. Encourage those who are timid. Take tender care of those who are weak. Be patient with everyone.

It's the day of the big game. The winner will go to the final four. The score is 1-1 going into the final few minutes, and there's only one player open for the shot. If only it wasn't Tommy Elkins.

Tommy's Shoes

Say a guy wanted to tell you about hate. And anger. And stupidity. Say he wanted to tell you about ignoring his dad's advice to be a light that shines for other people to see—and about finally listening to his dad's advice. If a guy had all this to tell, would you listen? Even if it came out in a mixed-up way because the guy telling you is 12 years old and better at soccer than putting the story into words?

You see, I love playing soccer. Every time I put on my jersey with *Sanchez* printed on the back, my veins start pulsing with the thrill of an upcoming game: the speed, the precision—all of it. So maybe you'll understand my frustration over a team member who just couldn't cut it. By the way, my first name's Roberto.

It first started one Saturday morning on the soccer field. I was standing behind the sideline at midfield, holding the ball over my head with both hands. This was a crucial throw-in. We were down one goal, with only one minute left in the game.

While losing the game would not knock us out of the play-offs, it wouldn't help. We wanted to finish in the top four, and a win or a tie would almost guarantee it.

With the ball above my head, I scanned the field. Our team wore blue jerseys. The other team wore red.

I looked for an open blue jersey. It wasn't easy. Red clogged the middle, taking away a direct attack. Red danced around, covering our blue.

I faked a throw one way, then I saw Steve Martindale break loose on the other side of the field.

Careful, I told myself. In pressure, it is too easy to make a mistake. I needed to keep both feet on the ground as I threw the ball. It might be routine in practice, but in a tournament, there is no such thing as routine.

Steve stopped, dashed forward, faked a move to the left, then spun back.

I was expecting that. Steve's my closest friend on the team. He's tall and skinny, and he has red hair that hangs over his eyes, so he wears a headband when he plays soccer.

I threw, knowing where Steve was headed. He didn't have to break stride as he reached the ball.

I didn't just stand and watch, though. I sprinted for an open space just behind him. I knew the ball was coming back to me on a give-and-go.

It did.

I trapped it with my right foot.

I knew I had about a second before a red forward was on me.

I pretended to mishandle the ball to give him confidence.

It worked. He overcommitted, hoping to strip me of the ball for a clear breakaway on our net.

I flipped the ball past the red player and reached it two steps later. Now, briefly, there were ten of us against nine of them.

I kept dribbling forward. Two reds peeled off to intercept me. It was all I needed.

Two blues were streaking for open positions upfield.

Time for a killer pass.

I knew it would catch the other team by surprise. For the whole game, I had been dumping the ball off immediately with short, safe passes. Not once had I shown the ability to bomb the ball.

I kept my head down, trying to fool them into thinking I hadn't seen two blue jerseys cut past their midfielders.

That gave me a choice. I could pass to John Harper, a great player with good feet, or I could pass to Tommy Elkins, total loser.

Easy choice, except their players knew it was an easy choice too, and a red jersey beelined to cover John.

That left Tommy Elkins, the coach's son. He was short and skinny and was blind without his contact lenses.

Do not pass to him, I told myself. *Do not pass to him. Do not pass to him.*

Tommy was one of the worst players to ever lace up soccer cleats. He had made the team only because his dad was the coach. Everybody knew that. And everybody thought he was a loser because of it.

Did I want to throw away a scoring chance by giving him the ball?

But I didn't have a choice. Tommy was the only one open.

So I made my best pass. With a quick, powerful swing

of my right foot, I served up a 40-yard cross-field pass with some left-to-right spin. As the ball made a banana curve through the air, high above the defenders, I knew I had laid it in perfectly.

Not only was Tommy open, but he had the advantage of a full sprint. The ball bounced into an open area just over their sweeper's shoulder. He tried to turn and stay with Tommy but didn't have a chance.

My pass put Tommy all alone on a breakaway, with only 20 steps between him and the goalie—and the net.

Tommy leaned into his kick, beat the goalie clean, and . . . missed the net by 20 feet. The ball bounced harmlessly out of play.

A clear breakaway. Goalie out of position. And no goal. What a loser.

The last half minute ticked away on our chance to tie the game.

I wasn't the only guy mad about it. As Tommy walked by the bench, we all made a point of ignoring him. "What a jerk," we mumbled back and forth, "forcing himself on the rest of us just because his dad is the coach."

Tommy walked alone to the parking lot.

▼ ▼ ▼ ▼ ▼

A few minutes later, I followed. The sun was shining brightly off the cars and the pavement, but I felt dark inside. I wanted two minutes with Tommy, and I was going to let him know what all of us on the team thought. Maybe that would fix the situation.

As I walked, I did my best to ignore my dad's voice. It kept echoing with the advice he had given me at breakfast as I complained about yet another game with Tommy Elkins.

"Play a game in Tommy's shoes," Dad had said. "Compassion isn't just a thing to talk about in church. Who you are needs to shine in everything you do."

Play a game in Tommy's shoes? *More like throw his shoes away for him,* I decided as I stomped toward his father's van. Dad would understand if he had seen how Tommy had blown an easy breakaway off my perfect pass.

When I reached the front of the van, Tommy already had the back hatch up, loading team equipment. But before I could reach Tommy, his father caught up to him at the rear of the van.

I stopped. What I wanted to say to Tommy was just between him and me. So I waited. Neither of them saw me at the front of the van.

"Clumsy fool!" Mr. Elkins half shouted. "How could you miss?"

"Dad," Tommy said, "I told you already, I'm no good at this. Won't you let me quit? That way I won't let the team down anymore."

"No son of mine is a quitter," Mr. Elkins said. "I was leading scorer when I played at your age, and I don't care what it takes—you'll do the same."

"But Dad . . . "

I backed away from the van before I heard the rest of what Tommy had to say in his sad voice. I didn't want them to see me. I'd already heard enough.

▼ ▼ ▼ ▼ ▼

The next game we played—a week later—was the one we absolutely had to win to make the final four. A tie wasn't good enough. I found Tommy for a little pregame pep talk. He looked hesitant when he saw me approach.

251

"Hey, Tommy," I began. His eyes shifted toward the ground, and he cleared his throat in what looked like nervousness. No doubt he wasn't expecting to hear something good. I continued. "Just wanted to give you a heads up to watch for me to pass it to you. Be ready, okay?"

Tommy looked up, and a flash of confusion passed over his face. He waited for more explanation but I left it at that. I just nodded with what I hoped he'd take as a boost of support and moved on to get ready for the game.

The game was a close one all the way through. At 1-1 going into the final few minutes, we desperately needed a goal.

Down at their end, Steve and I passed the ball back and forth until I saw John Harper open. I dumped it to him. He kicked the ball hard, but his shot bounced off their defender and out-of-bounds.

Corner kick.

Forty-five seconds left.

We lined up quickly.

Their team—all brown uniforms—formed a wall of defense in front of their net.

Steve took position in the corner to kick it in.

He lofted the ball high. As it came down, one of their strikers broke away from the wall of defense to boot the ball toward midfield. John Harper fought him for it, and the striker's kick wobbled the ball weakly toward me.

I trapped it and looked up. Two brown uniforms were dashing toward me.

There was no place to go but to Tommy. He was hanging to the left side of the net, alone and unguarded because no one ever worried about him. All the defensemen were on the other side of the goal.

All I needed to do was get the ball to him in the air . . .

I faked a pass to my right, enough to get both attackers leaning that direction. Then, with a flick of my foot, I chipped the ball toward the left goalpost.

It hung against the sky briefly. As it dropped, Tommy timed his jump perfectly. He slammed his head forward, and caught the ball flush in the center of his forehead.

The goalie didn't have a chance. The ball caught the underside of the crossbar and dropped in behind the goalie's shoulder.

Goal! Two to one! We were in the final four!

All of us on the field danced around, hugging and screaming!

In all that noise and celebrating, Tommy pulled himself out from under a pile of people and looked for me.

He got close to my ear and spoke so that nobody could hear him. "Remember what you said to me at the beginning of the game?" he said. "That I should be on the lookout . . . "

" . . . for the perfect time to give you the perfect pass?" I asked.

He nodded, so happy he was almost crying. "It was kind of like if a good player like you believed I could do it, it helped me believe in myself."

"No big deal," I said. I grinned. "What size shoes do you have?"

He frowned, puzzled. "Eight and a half," he said. "Why do you want to know?"

"Funny," I said, understanding better what it meant to put myself in someone else's shoes. "Mine are eight and a half, too. Perfect fit."

He didn't understand what I meant. But it didn't matter. Because I did.

WHAT'S UP THIS WEEK?

- Compassion vs. Criticism
- More than Meets the Eye
- The Power of Encouragement

PRAYER POWER

Are you an encouraging person? Or is it easier for you to see the faults in others? If you're like most people, it's easier to see the faults. Ask God to prepare your heart to learn from him this week.

COMPASSION VS. CRITICISM

Let's admit it: It's easier to be critical than compassionate. Most of us can find any number of things wrong with people. We get impatient when they don't fit into our ideals or plans. Today let's focus on changing a critical spirit into one of compassion.

BRAIN STRETCHERS

FOR KIDS:

1. In "Tommy's Shoes," what does everyone think about Tommy?
2. Have you ever felt unaccepted by anyone? How did that make you feel?

ASK AN ADULT:

1. Has anyone ever criticized you too much? How did that make you feel?
2. Have you ever shown compassion to someone who didn't fit in? Tell about it.
3. Does it ever seem easier for you to be critical than compassionate? Why?

SCRIPTURE POWER

Honest words are painful, but what do your criticisms amount to? (Job 6:25)

It's easy to find faults in other people. No one is perfect, and we tend to focus on the bad things in others. But what good does that do? It simply makes us unpleasant people with negative attitudes. And it causes pain and insecurity in the people we criticize.

Don't speak evil against each other, my dear brothers and sisters. If you criticize each other and condemn each other, then you are criticizing and condemning God's law. (James 4:11)

When we think someone is a loser, we are thinking exactly the opposite of what God thinks. "Losers" are people that God values very highly—so much so that he sent Jesus to die so that everyone, including people like that, could live. Perhaps we should put ourselves in those people's shoes and then start treating them differently. Who knows— maybe we'll be able to help them see that they can be winners too.

Anyone who harms you harms my most precious possession. (Zechariah 2:8)

Each person is God's most precious possession. When we criticize someone, we harm that person— someone very special whom God holds dear to his heart. He sees more in each of us than we see in ourselves or in each other. Since God places such high value on each person he creates, how can we treat someone poorly?

*Stop criticizing others, or it will all come back on you.
(Luke 6:37)*

This verse warns of one consequence of our criticism: eventually we will be treated with the same critical spirit that we use with others. Would you want to be treated the way you treat others?

So also, the tongue is a small thing, but what enormous damage it can do. A tiny spark can set a great forest on fire. . . . Sometimes it praises our Lord and Father, and sometimes it breaks out into curses against those who have been made in the image of God. (James 3:5, 9)

If we claim to be Christians, we have a responsibility to use our words carefully toward others. We've each been made in the image of God, and that makes every person worth treating with the utmost kindness and compassion.

The Lord is good to everyone. He showers compassion on all his creation. (Psalm 145:9)

God sets the example for us with his compassion. The verse above says he "showers" compassion on everything. That's more than just a trickle or a drip of compassion. He's serious about dousing us with it! And he wants us to do the same for others.

PRAYER POWER

Look closely at your actions toward the people with whom you find it easiest to be critical. Do you struggle with a critical spirit? Is there someone who gets on your nerves because he or she just doesn't fit in? If so, then talk to God about it, and ask him to work on this area of your heart.

WEDNESDAY

MORE THAN MEETS THE EYE

"There is more to people than meets the eye." Have you ever heard that saying? It means that once we look deeper into why people are the way they are, we often find reasons that help us understand and be less critical. Let's check this out a little more.

BRAIN STRETCHERS

FOR KIDS:

1. How do you think God would feel about Roberto's view of Tommy at the beginning of this week's story?
2. How did Roberto's attitude toward Tommy change after catching a glimpse of the pressure Tommy's dad put on his son?
3. How do you think you would have reacted to Tommy when he missed the shot?

ASK AN ADULT:

1. Why do you suppose God gives some people certain skills and not others?
2. Have you ever had a bad opinion about someone but thought differently once you got to know him or her better?

SCRIPTURE POWER

He found them in a desert land, in an empty, howling wasteland. He surrounded them and watched over them; he guarded them as his most precious possession. (Deuteronomy 32:10)

The world places value on people because of what they can do, rather than who they are. Because of this, people who can't perform to a certain standard suddenly seem of less value. But God sees each person as precious. He sees beyond the surface and loves each of us unconditionally, in spite of our weaknesses.

O God, whom I praise, don't stand silent and aloof while the wicked slander me and tell lies about me. They are all around me with their hateful words, and they fight against me for no reason. . . . I am an object of mockery to people everywhere; when they see me, they shake their heads. Help me, O Lord my God! Save me because of your unfailing love. . . . For he stands beside the needy, ready to save them from those who condemn them. (Psalm 109:1-3, 25-26, 31)

King David wrote this psalm when he was feeling mocked and misunderstood by his enemies. But he trusted God to define his identity. It didn't matter whether other people just looked at the surface. There was so much more to him than what they saw. It's a mistake to assume we know all about a person. There is always more than meets the eye. Sometimes our opinions of others change when we take the time to look at life through their eyes, or when we "stand in their shoes."

Is there any encouragement from belonging to Christ? Any comfort from his love? Any fellowship together in the Spirit? Are your hearts tender and sympathetic? Then make me truly happy by agreeing wholeheartedly with each other, loving one another, and working together with one heart and purpose. (Philippians 2:1-2)

The above verses show a desire for unity and togetherness. Just like a soccer team, Christians make up a team. And on any team, unity and understanding are essential. A team is only as strong as its individual members. There isn't room for quick criticisms and judgments of others. Really working together, looking beyond the surface, and learning what makes another person tick is key to strengthening the team.

PRAYER POWER

Spend a few minutes in quietness with God. Ask him to let you know if you've been too quick to make a decision about someone else. Commit to looking beyond the surface and finding out what could be "more than meets the eye" about the people in your life.

THE POWER OF ENCOURAGEMENT

We've all probably felt the energy of someone's positive words. Tommy sure did the day he won the soccer game. Encouragement is invigorating and energizing! Let's look closer at this topic.

BRAIN STRETCHERS
FOR KIDS:

1. Do you think Tommy probably felt like an outsider on the team? How did Roberto's encouraging words help Tommy?
2. Has there ever been a time when you've encouraged someone and it's had a positive result?

ASK AN ADULT:

1. Why do people need encouragement?
2. What are some encouraging things people have said about you? In what ways has that helped you?

SCRIPTURE POWER

He will not crush those who are weak or quench the smallest hope.

He will bring full justice to all who have been wronged. (Isaiah 42:3)

God is on the side of people who are weak or don't have hope. If you ever feel like you fit into that category, think about the power of the God of the universe backing you! And, if you're ever tempted to criticize someone for being weak or incapable, this verse is a great reminder of God's viewpoint.

So encourage each other and build each other up. . . . Encourage those who are timid. Take tender care of those who are weak. Be patient with everyone. (1 Thessalonians 5:11, 14)

In a nutshell, our actions and attitude toward weaker people should be those of patience and compassion.

The heartfelt counsel of a friend is as sweet as perfume and incense. (Proverbs 27:9)

Have you ever felt the boost of a friend's encouraging words? Encouragement is a powerful force, providing strength and motivation to reach higher and move beyond what we believe our capabilities are. Tommy's goal at the end of the story is just one example of the energy behind encouragement.

When you have repented and turned to me again, strengthen and build up your brothers. (Luke 22:32)

Roberto did the right thing by seeing the error of his critical thinking about Tommy. He realized he had made a judgment based on less than all the facts. Through Roberto's choice to live out the above verse, God built up Tommy's confidence and blessed the whole team that day.

PRAYER POWER
While you're praying today, ask God to show you how to be an encourager. Also ask him to put people on your mind who need the boost of your encouraging words. Tell God you want to make it a goal to be known as someone who builds up others.

CONCLUDING THOUGHTS

In "Tommy's Shoes," nobody likes Tommy because he is a lousy soccer player. He can't seem to do anything right, and because he didn't score on a breakaway, the team might not have made it into the play-offs. It would be easy to point out Tommy's faults, and it might even seem like he deserves it. It's a lot harder for us to try on someone else's shoes—to really try to understand what that person is going through. It's much easier to let him know what a loser you think he is.

Like the rest of the team, Roberto was furious at Tommy for jeopardizing their chances to make it to the final four. But when he overheard the real reason Tommy plays soccer, Roberto felt more understanding toward his teammate. He chose a strategic move to build up Tommy's confidence—he encouraged him and told him to be ready for the perfect pass. That opportunity came in the next game, and Tommy's strengthened confidence helped him score the winning goal.

Every person is made up of so much

more than what others can see at first glance. Sometimes we can be surprised with unexpected friends when we make the effort to look beyond the surface, to walk in their shoes, and to discover "more than meets the eye."

Are you willing to look beyond the surface?

LINE IT UP!

Become an encourager. Habits are developed through practice, and developing the habit of being an encourager is simple. All you have to do is make a point to say at least one encouraging thing to someone every day. Make sure it's sincere, of course. You'll be amazed at the positive attitude that comes from building up others.

PRAYER POWER

In today's prayer time, thank God for all the ways he encourages you in his Word. If you need encouragement today, flip through the Psalms, find one that fits with a situation you're facing, and pray it out loud. Pouring out your thoughts to God in prayer will keep your mind focused on his priorities and will give you the desire to encourage others.

WEEK 14

WHAT'S UP THIS WEEK:
Sold Out for Jesus

THEME VERSES FOR THE WEEK:
Luke 14:26-27

[Jesus said,] "If you want to be my follower you must love me more than your own father and mother, wife and children, brothers and sisters—yes, more than your own life. Otherwise, you cannot be my disciple. And you cannot be my disciple if you do not carry your own cross and follow me."

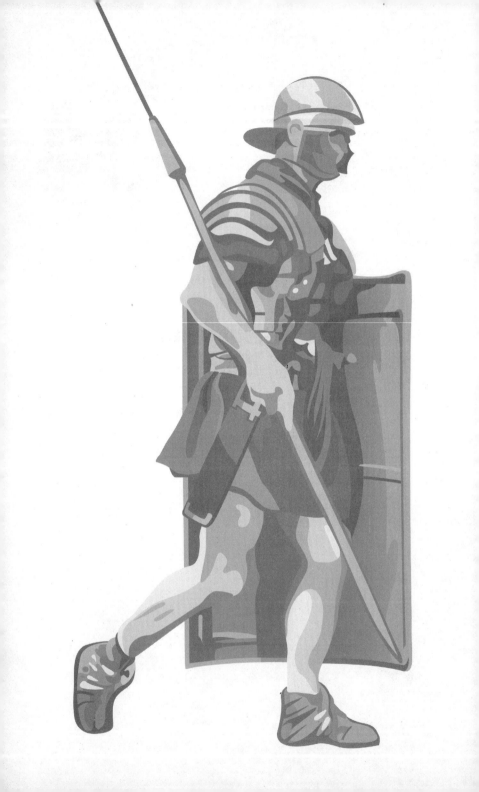

*Secret hideouts, dark passageways, and
furtive glances to see who could be
following—lurking around the next
corner. . . . That is the life Claudius and
his family have been thrown into to
escape the power of an evil emperor.
How much are they willing to give up
for their faith in Jesus?*

Historical Note: The Roman emperor Galerius
was one of the most fanatical in his determination to persecute followers of Christ. Beginning
in A.D. 303, his soldiers tortured and killed thousands and thousands of believers. Yet on his
deathbed in A.D. 311, Galerius acknowledged
defeat and, indeed, did ask the Christians for
their prayers. While Claudius and Theo, identi-
fied in the story as sons of a senator, do not
appear in the history books, it is entirely plausi-
ble that in their generation the yearly celebration of Jesus' birth spread to other families, for
the first mention of the celebration of Christmas
occurs in A.D. 336 in an early Roman calendar.

Catacomb Glory

Claudius stood at the side of the fish
stand as he waited for the old woman
and the grown man to notice him.

"Rumors on the streets say Galerius is
on his deathbed," the man was saying.
"Who shall be emperor next?"

"Bah," the old woman replied. "He will be a fool, for only a fool would want the headaches of the Roman empire."

She shook her head from side to side in disgust, a movement that brought Claudius into her field of vision. She studied him for a few seconds.

"What fine clothes you wear!" she finally cackled. "Where did you steal them, boy?"

Claudius squared his shoulders and looked the crone directly in the eyes. "I can assure you I am no thief."

At his words, her coughing cackles ended abruptly. She peered at Claudius. "By the shades of Saturn, boy, I might believe you. Your accent—it's as if you were schooled among the rich."

The man with her sneered. "He walks these slums unattended? He hardly appears to be more than 12 harvests old."

Claudius remained straight and dignified. "My age is of no matter. I have silver, and I wish to purchase fish."

He opened his hand and showed her the glint of his coins.

The old crone opened her mouth to squawk, but for once, she was speechless. Such wealth! And in the hands of such a dove, ready to be plucked.

Claudius shifted his weight from one foot to the other. He did not enjoy it here in the strangeness of the marketplace. There was too much noise, too much activity—and the smells: rotting vegetables, the odors of unwashed bodies. . . . How he longed for the quiet of the summer villa which overlooked the sea. Yet if he did not secure food . . .

The crone was beckoning him forward.

"It's fish you want, boy? Look at this. The freshest in the market."

Claudius stepped forward and looked down into the

wooden bin. Flies crawled everywhere. The fish had been handled so roughly that half had been scraped of their scales. Yet if he did not secure food . . .

Claudius yelped. A pair of rough hands had grabbed his arms. The man had moved behind him and was pulling him in close.

"The silver, boy," he grunted. "Drop the silver and you'll be free to run."

The crone had a fish knife in her hand and a greedy smile on her face. "In these markets, boy, you're a fool to carry it. We're just helping you out."

She moved closer and waved the knife.

Claudius reacted without thinking. He kicked her in the shins, then he stamped downward on the man's toes. The woman squealed in anger, and the man roared in pain. In the confusion, Claudius twisted loose and ran. He dodged wagons and donkeys and soldiers and stands of fruit, and he ran until he was out of breath. Only then did he look behind him to see if he was free.

No pursuit.

He sobbed for breath.

No food either.

Claudius wanted to cry. Mamma and Theo waited, hungry and scared and helpless. Pappa? Well, Pappa had probably already been thrown to the lions.

Claudius clenched his fists, remembering what he'd first heard at the fish stand: Galerius was on his deathbed. Served the old tyrant right. Claudius hoped the emperor would die a slow and horrible death. If it weren't for Galerius, they would still be living the life of luxury accorded to a senator and his family, with a summer villa by the sea and a winter mansion here in Rome.

Claudius began to walk again, hardly seeing where his footsteps took him.

Just a month ago, Mamma and Pappa had taken the bath they insisted on calling a baptism.

"Baptism into what?" little Theo had asked.

"Into life with the one God," Mamma had replied with a smile.

"Not Jupiter or Mithras?"

"No," Pappa had said to Theo, "the true God, who sent his son to be born into this world over 300 years ago in a small town at the edge of the empire, a town called Bethlehem."

Claudius kept thinking about the conversation as he walked. After all, because of it, soldiers had marched to the mansion and taken Pappa away.

Pappa had told a wonderful story, about wise men bringing gifts to a baby in a manger—and about the miracles this Jesus had done as he grew older. Claudius knew the stories were important, for why else would Pappa have let the soldiers take him to the Colosseum, where lions waited to tear him apart?

At that thought, tears escaped Claudius's eyes. He immediately wiped them away.

When his sight cleared, he discovered that his aimless walking had not been so aimless after all. His feet had taken him into the hills of Rome, not far from his family's mansion.

It won't hurt, he told himself, *to have one last look at my old home before I retrace my steps to the market to find some food for Mamma and Theo . . .*

▼ ▼ ▼ ▼ ▼

"Mamma," Claudius called softly. "Mamma?"

Even with the safety from soldiers offered by these deep

tunnels, Claudius did not enjoy the catacomb cemetery, an underground maze of narrow passages dug into soft lava rock. Claudius was already two levels down, and from what Mamma had told him, he knew the tunnels were ancient and had hidden many generations of believers from cruel Roman emperors.

"Mamma," he called again, suddenly fearing that his painstakingly memorized directions had failed him. To be lost underground . . .

"Claudius!"

He hurried ahead until a turn in the tunnel brought him to his mother's voice. The shimmering light of an oil lamp showed her standing up straight, with little Theo hugging her leg. Here, the tunnel had been carved into a shallow bowl, giving them enough room to lay down a blanket for each of them. The oil lamp burned day and night, for if they put it out to sleep, they would have no way to light it again. Clay jugs held water and more lamp oil, and a basket held bread and dried figs, the last of their food.

Yet now Claudius had his arms full.

"What is this, son?" Mamma asked. For even in the dim light, it was clear that Claudius carried a great load. "I sent you for food."

Claudius smiled. "No food," he said. "Only gifts."

"Gifts?" Mamma put an arm around little Theo. "We cannot eat gifts."

"Mamma, would I do you wrong?" Claudius said in mock hurt, for now he was enjoying himself and the secret he had. "Can we not celebrate?"

"Celebrate? Claudius, we face death!"

"Why, Mamma? Because of the one born in Bethlehem?"

"Yes, Claudius, but—"

"Tell me the story again, Mamma, about wise men and angels singing. About miracles."

"But Claudius—"

"Please, Mamma?"

She could see that Claudius would have it no other way, so she sat down and told her sons the story. Her face softened with growing joy as she spoke each passing word, and when she finished, they kept a precious silence as each imagined the baby boy Jesus in that small town so far away in time and distance. In the depths of the catacombs, it was a silence so deep that it had power which matched the story Mamma had whispered.

Finally, Claudius spoke. "These gifts, then, Mamma, are to celebrate Jesus' birthday. We cannot bring gifts to him in a manger, so we give to each other and remember him."

"Tomorrow, then, you return to the market for food." Mamma smiled. "Today we think of Bethlehem. What a wonderful idea, son."

"It was not mine," Claudius said. He was bursting to share his secret.

"It was mine," a deeper voice announced from the darkness outside their lamplight.

Mamma leaped to her feet as a man walked into the light.

"Pappa," Theo cried in disbelief. He ran to his father and threw himself into his arms. "You defeated the lions!"

Pappa laughed. "No, Theo, I was released. Yesterday."

"How can that be?" Mamma asked. "And why . . . why . . . " Mamma couldn't find the strength to finish her question.

Claudius knew the answer. He, too, had been stunned with disbelief to see Pappa, sitting on the edge of the steps of the mansion. He had been overjoyed at the chance to lead his father back to Mamma and Theo here in the catacombs.

And he had listened to the miracle which Pappa was now explaining.

"To those who do not understand the meaning of Jesus' birth," Pappa was saying to Mamma and Theo, "death is frightening beyond compare. Galerius now faces death, and it is that fear which brought him to what we once believed was impossible. Galerius has halted the persecution and asked all Christians for their prayers. He will die in peace."

Pappa hugged his family again. "I never knew if I would find you again, and I waited and waited, hoping one of you might return, perhaps to sneak into the mansion for some of our silver or possessions. Today, Claudius appeared—in answer to my prayers."

"A double miracle," Mamma said as she held Pappa. "Truly worthy of a celebration of Jesus' birth."

Little Theo laughed and clapped his hands with glee. "A birthday for Jesus! Can we do it again after the next harvest?"

WHAT'S UP THIS WEEK?
- Count the Cost
- Persecuted
- Worth It All

PRAYER POWER

Being sold out for Jesus is something not many people choose. It can be costly, but it is the only way to live fully. God has a great adventure in store for those who give him their whole heart. Pray and talk to God about your excitement, hesitations, concerns, doubts, and hopes about taking the risk of being sold out for him. Trust that he'll show you some things this week that will prepare you for the great adventure he has planned for you.

COUNT THE COST

Being sold out for Jesus first requires us to think about the seriousness of that commitment. We don't know right now what he'll ask us to face. All we know is that he asks for our all.

BRAIN STRETCHERS

FOR KIDS:

1. What kind of lifestyle did Claudius and his family have before they had to go into hiding? (Keep in mind what his father did for a living.)
2. How do you think Jesus felt about their willingness to give everything up for him?

ASK AN ADULT:

1. Have there been things in your life that you've had to let go of because you wanted to be sold out for God? What were those things?
2. Have you ever had to choose between pleasing God and pleasing a person? What happened?

SCRIPTURE POWER

It is dangerous to make a rash promise to God before counting the cost. (Proverbs 20:25)

What does God want from us? Well, he wants everything. He wants to be our top priority. But he doesn't want us to promise him things we aren't willing to back up with action. Just like we want our friends and family to keep their promises, God wants us to be trustworthy and to mean what we say to him.

> [Jesus said,] "If you want to be my follower you must love me more than your own father and mother, wife and children, brothers and sisters—yes, more than your own life. Otherwise, you cannot be my disciple. And you cannot be my disciple if you do not carry your own cross and follow me. But don't begin until you count the cost. For who would begin construction of a building without first getting estimates and then checking to see if there is enough money to pay the bills? Otherwise, you might complete only the foundation before running out of funds. And then how everyone would laugh at you! They would say, 'There's the person who started that building and ran out of money before it was finished!' Or what king would ever dream of going to war without first sitting down with his counselors and discussing whether his army of ten thousand is strong enough to defeat the twenty thousand soldiers who are marching against him? If he is not able, then while the enemy is still far away, he will send a delegation to discuss terms of peace. So no one can become my disciple without giving up everything for me." (Luke 14:26-33)

Walking blindly into challenges is a sure way to lose. And entering the Christian life is no different. Jesus asks for faithful followers, but he warns us to consider the cost that a life of obedience will bring. Counting the cost means being prepared for the hardships and rejection that may come from others who do not understand or welcome the good news of Jesus' salvation. Sometimes that rejection can come from people we love most of all, whether they're family members or friends. God certainly doesn't want us to stop loving them, but he does want us to choose him first. Don't worry, though. The payoff will be so worth it. Just wait until Thursday, and we'll look at why following Jesus is worth it all.

PRAYER POWER

Talk to God today about counting the cost of living for him. You may have already dealt with this a bit in your life. Ask him to show you each day how his strength will be all the help you need to live the life he calls you to live. He can be counted on!

PERSECUTED

Yesterday we touched a little on rejection that can come from people around us because of our faith in Jesus. Another word for that is *persecution*. We'll look at that more today.

BRAIN STRETCHERS
FOR KIDS:

1. What do you think Claudius learned from watching his father's willingness to die for his faith in Jesus? Do you think Claudius's faith was strengthened? Why or why not?

2. If you're a Christian, how do your friends and other kids at school feel about that? Are you ever tempted to avoid letting people know about your faith?

ASK AN ADULT:

1. Do you know of any missionaries or people from other countries who have been arrested or killed because they were Christians? Does that thought scare you?

2. Why does the world hate Christians?

3. Have you ever been criticized or made fun of because of your faith? If so, how did you react?

SCRIPTURE POWER

The apostles left the high council rejoicing that God had counted them worthy to suffer dishonor for the name of Jesus. And every day, in the Temple and in their homes, they continued to teach and preach this message: "The Messiah you are looking for is Jesus." (Acts 5:41-42)

Christians are still persecuted today. Thousands are put to death because they refuse to renounce their faith in Christ. And even if we don't risk dying because we are Christians, it can be difficult to stand up for our faith when we know people will make fun of us or exclude us. Rejection is never easy, so there may be times when it's a challenge to stand up for what we believe.

Don't be surprised, dear brothers and sisters, if the world hates you. (1 John 3:13)

The Bible assures us that we will be persecuted for our faith. That's not one of the promises we like to put on our fridge as a reminder to live by, but it is a promise just the same. The promise is there so we won't be surprised when it happens—and so we'll be ready to stand up for God when we're tempted to walk away from our faith. God promises that he will be with us in those situations and will give us the strength to handle whatever comes our way. Even for persecuted Christians being put to death, there is great hope in knowing that they are leaving this imperfect world and going to be with our heavenly Father in glory.

When the world hates you, remember it hated me before it hated you. The world would love you if you belonged to it, but you don't. I chose you to come out of the world, and so it hates you. Do you remember what I told you? "A servant is not greater than the master." Since they persecuted me, naturally they will persecute you. And if they had listened to me, they would listen to you! The people of the world will hate you because you belong to me, for they don't know God who sent me. (John 15:18-21)

We are not alone in the Christian life. Jesus did nothing wrong, loved all people, and did everything he could to reconcile people to God. In spite of that, the world hated him! It shouldn't be a surprise to us, then, when the world isn't too excited that we follow Christ. Our example puts pressure on them to consider sacrificing their sinful ways and serving God. God's truth has a way of angering people who are happy to keep on sinning. And when we stand up for that truth, we are putting ourselves directly in the path of their anger. But there's hope. Jesus won the victory over sin, and he promises that those who choose him above all else will be blessed beyond what anyone can imagine.

PRAYER POWER

No one can understand persecution better than Jesus. He is ready and willing to hear your hurts when you don't fit in because you choose to obey him. Tell him what's on your mind. He'll be the strength you need to keep on with your walk of faith.

WORTH IT ALL

Let's get to the good news now! Living sold out for Jesus means giving him your all. And it is worth it—without a doubt, hands down, no contest! It is the absolute best way to live. Let's definitely spend some time finding out why.

BRAIN STRETCHERS
FOR KIDS:

1. "Catacomb Glory" has a happy ending. Would it still have been a good ending if Claudius and his family had died for their faith? What would they have gained then?

2. Has there been a time in your life when you've chosen to stand up for Jesus and you've experienced a positive result? How did you feel, knowing God was pleased with you? If you had it to do over again, would you make the same right choice?

ASK AN ADULT:

1. How has living for Jesus been worth it all for you?

2. What would you say to someone who is having trouble deciding whether to live sold out for Jesus?

SCRIPTURE POWER

Don't be afraid of what you are about to suffer. The Devil will throw some of you into prison and put you to the test. You will be persecuted for "ten days." Remain faithful even when facing death, and I will give you the crown of life. (Revelation 2:10)

God blesses those who are persecuted because they live for God, for the Kingdom of Heaven is theirs. (Matthew 5:10)

Persecuted Christians can be happy in difficult times. Though it is not easy, we know we are on the right track when we face difficulties, because that's how the world treats those who serve God. We are promised a great reward in heaven if we stand firm in our faith.

Look, I am coming quickly. Hold on to what you have, so that no one will take away your crown. (Revelation 3:11)

When that day arrives, the Lord their God will rescue his people, just as a shepherd rescues his sheep. They will sparkle in his land like jewels in a crown. (Zechariah 9:16)

As Christians, we have hope that goes beyond what anyone can say or do to us or take from us. We know that Jesus will make everything right in the end, and our place in eternity is secure with him. We need to keep encouraging each other to hold on to the faith we have in Christ. When Jesus returns, we will know without a doubt that our faithfulness was the right move. No regrets!

PRAYER POWER

Have you experienced God's peace when you've chosen to follow him despite watching others around you who are going their own way? Has that encouraged you to make the right decision again the next time you are faced with a similar situation? Ask God to prepare you to be strong for that next time. Thank him for the ways he'll make following him worth it all for you.

CONCLUDING THOUGHTS

In "Catacomb Glory," Christians were being persecuted because of their faith in Christ. Claudius was scared because his family was in hiding in the catacombs and fearful for their lives, and he thought his father had already been put to death because he was a Christian.

Claudius and his family were spared death, but even if they hadn't been, they understood that God was with them. It is better to die with Christ than to live without him. That was something that Galerius didn't know, and even though he had wealth and power, he was terrified as he faced death.

Choosing to be sold out for God won't be easy. But it's been said that anything worthwhile takes some effort. The adventure of faith is one that a lot of people choose not to live. God has given us the gift of his Word, which is filled with stories of brave people who did choose to give up everything for him. And if they could speak to us from where they are today, they certainly would tell us to accept God's challenge. They have found it to be worth it all.

LINE IT UP!

Pull out that personal mission statement from a few weeks ago (on page 122). Anything you want to add? Maybe you're feeling fired up from this week's challenging lesson. Add a prayer to your mission statement, telling God where you are in regard to letting go and accepting the journey of being sold out for him. Hang on to that piece of paper. Do you want to make God proud years from now when you can look at the paper and know that you've walked the path he had for you? Consider the costs, and choose Jesus!

PRAYER POWER

This week may have been tough to take. We did lots of thinking and considering just what God may require of you as you live for him. Are you up for the adventure? Ask him to make your heart courageous. Expect his help; he will honor your request to please him. Make him number one!

WHAT'S UP THIS WEEK:
True Courage

THEME VERSE FOR THE WEEK:
1 John 2:28

And now, dear children, continue to live
in fellowship with Christ so that when he
returns, you will be full of courage and not
shrink back from him in shame.

We've all had heroes in our life. A hero is courageous and strong, willing to speak up and fight for what's right. Seth thinks he knows what it is to be a hero. He's about to learn more.

Editor's Note: This story is longer than the other weeks' stories. However, it's a great one! Plan some extra time to read it.

Buffalo Soldier

Wyoming Territory, Laramie, December 1874

I didn't have to call out farther than to the front of the church for Pa. Good thing, too. I could hardly speak with the revolver barrel pressed hard against my cheekbone.

"I'm a man in a desperate situation," the man behind the revolver said. "We'll just wait easy 'til your pappy gits here."

"Yes, sir," I said. "He's just setting candles up at the pulpit."

Pa was setting candles. I had been forced to hang Christmas decorations here in the church foyer. In other words, if I was on my own, beholden to no one, this wouldn't have happened. Instead, I had looked up at a sudden blast of wind to see the man stumble through the doorway, blizzard snow swirling around his overcoat. He was what the Sioux called a buffalo soldier—a former slave who had fought in the army against them. Without a word the man had kicked the door shut, pointed a Colt .45 at my head, walked up and spun me around, wrapped his arm around my neck, pressed the gun to my face, and backed us up to a wall.

This did not bode well for my plans. I had a train ticket in my pocket—I'd saved six months on the sly for it—and was intending to leave town directly, while Pa was distracted with preaching over the Christmas season.

"What is it, Seth?" Pa's voice reached us before he did. His eyes widened as he stepped into the foyer and saw the two of us.

"Easy now, preacher man," the man behind me said. "This ain't what it appears."

For a moment, Pa studied us. Gusts of wind broke the silence by rattling the stained-glass windows. I barely dared breathe.

"Let my son be," Pa finally said to the man holding me hostage. "Whatever you care to discuss in the house of the Lord don't need a gun."

This was my pa? He stood up straight in his black suit, with calm, clear eyes and a calm, clear voice. I'd never figured him to be brave. He was a Bible-waving preacher, not the pistol-toting marshal I wanted to be someday.

"I'm calling upon the sanctuary of this church to protect me," the buffalo soldier said. "Until you hear me out, I got your boy."

Before Pa could reply, the church door slammed open again. Five men pushed their way inside, with the wind pushing from behind, sending flurries of snow dancing at their boots.

It took them several seconds to understand the situation. By then, Pa had moved directly in front of me and the man.

"Stand aside, Reverend. We're here for the buffalo soldier," said the man in the center, holding a rifle waist-high pointed directly at us.

"No," Pa said, still calm and clear. "You men either set your guns down or go on home."

"This soldier just shot Mayor Crawford. We caught him standing overtop, ready to rob the mayor. We're here to make sure he hangs."

"He has called upon the Lord for protection," Pa answered. "As long as he remains in the Lord's house, he shall not hang."

"Reverend." The man's voice held impatience. Because folks would be arriving for Christmas Eve service within the hour, we'd piled the stove with coal and it was considerable warm. Melted snow dripped water from the man's hat brim onto the floor. "I told you once. Stand aside or—"

"Or you'll shoot?" Pa asked. "Five armed men, gunning down a preacher?"

Despite my own fear, I marveled at the strength in Pa's voice.

"Reverend . . . " another one began. "What Riley is saying is—"

"Turn around gentlemen. Keep guard outside if you like. While this man is inside the church, he is protected." Pa's voice lost some of its steel. "You have my word. I will not help him escape."

The five men took turns looking at one another, until the leader grudgingly backed up and led them into the cold again.

Pa waited until the door closed behind them, then he turned to us. "Let my son be."

The pressure of the buffalo soldier's arm dropped from my throat. He pushed me away. I was able to stand beside Pa and get my first close look.

"What's your name, brother?" Pa asked.

"Silas Freeman," he said in a croak. "Ninth Cavalry. I didn't shoot no mayor."

I'd only heard of buffalo soldiers but had never seen one, nor any other man with skin so dark. His was burnished black, like the leather cover of my pa's Bible. He had tightly-curled, dark hair, cropped short. He was covered by a great overcoat. And at his feet there was a puddle of blood.

"Fact is, preacher, I heard shots in the alley. I run in, find a man lying in his blood, and see three men running away. I kneel down, hoping to assist him. I stand and shout for help, and the three men turn back. Before I can say a word, one man—the one named Riley—lifts his rifle and shoots me. It made more sense to run than get kilt."

As I watched, the man's Colt dropped from his hand. "Don't let me die," Silas said, his voice fading. "My woman and my baby are coming in tonight on the train. I'm on my first leave from Fort Sanders. We was going to have our first Christmas together."

He swayed briefly, then he began to fall. Pa stepped forward and caught the man.

"Help me set him down gentle," Pa said, grunting with the effort of holding the larger man.

We laid the man on his back. Pa opened the man's overcoat. We saw a great red stain spreading across the blue of his soldier's uniform. "Run, get Doc Harper," Pa told me. "This man's been shot bad."

▼ ▼ ▼ ▼ ▼

"It's the preacher's boy, Seth Brown," someone called out. "He's come looking for Doc Harper."

I stood in a crowd of people gathered in the parlor room at the Crawford house. I'd been directed here to look for Doc.

"Ain't someone told him about the shooting?" someone called back. "Doc's real busy with the mayor."

Sweat and melting snow ran down my face. It had been a hard run through the blizzard. Here in the parlor room—with all the folks worried about someone as important as Mayor Crawford—it hardly seemed there was air to breathe. And back at the church, a man was dying.

So I stepped ahead, politely asking to get through. At the bedroom door, a wide man blocked my path. Pa and I had only been in town a few months—we'd buried Ma and two sisters to pneumonia back in Maine—but I recognized the man as Deputy Marshal Jake Wilson.

"Sorry, son," he said, his voice kind. "Just kinfolk allowed inside."

"Yes, sir," I said. "Only there's a man by the name of Silas Freeman back at the church. He's been shot too."

"We'll send someone to fetch him here, I reckon."

"Sir, he c'ain't leave the church. There's other men outside the church waiting to gun him down."

"Son?"

I explained.

Jake frowned. "Jethro Riley didn't say nothing about seeing no man robbing the mayor. Otherwise I'd be out looking instead of standing here. And son, if I was there, it wouldn't be no lynch mob. Just a plain and simple arrest."

"Jethro Riley?" I said. "Silas Freeman said a man named Riley shot him! And there was a Riley at the church!"

"Must be one of the brothers. Frank or Adam. Jethro's still here across the parlor." Jake rapped on the door behind him. "Sam," he called to the marshal, "best you git out here."

As the door opened, I caught a glimpse of a stooped older man, Doc Harper, among those gathered round the bed. Marshal Keaton stepped out of the bedroom.

Since finding out we would be moving to Wyoming Territory from Maine, all I'd done was read adventures about the Wild West. Here was a man who seemed to be straight from one of my Wild West novels—someone I'd be like soon enough.

He was a tall, lean man with dark hair, blue eyes, and a scar across his cheek. I'd heard plenty on how he'd bested more than his share of crooks. A real-life Wild West hero. I'd always wanted to introduce myself, but I was too shy.

"Jake?" The marshal looked over at his deputy.

"Listen to this young man, Sam. This is Seth Brown. The preacher's boy."

I told the story again, calm as I could. Marshal Keaton nodded. Didn't spend much time in thought.

"Jake, seems like the reverend is living up to the reputation that preceded him and don't need much help, but you best make tracks out to the church anyway. Take Doc Harper. Appears Doc's done all he can for Crawford for now."

Keaton moved his blue eyes to mine. "Seth, how 'bout you ride with me to the Riley spread. I've got questions for you, but there's no time to waste. We'll talk as we ride."

"Yes, sir," I said. "Yes, sir!"

▼ ▼ ▼ ▼ ▼

We didn't have time to get me a horse, and Marshal Keaton said it weren't far anyhow, so we shared the marshal's, a big red roan. I was glad to have the marshal ahead of me and blocking the fierce gusts of snow as we rode.

"Tell me about this Silas Freeman," Marshal Keaton said, turning his head and raising his voice to be heard above the wind. "Was he carrying anything?"

"Just a gun, sir." I leaned forward and described how he'd entered the church and what he looked like.

"He said he saw three men in the alley? But there was five by the time he got to the church."

"Yes, sir. I understood they'd gathered in a hurry to chase down Silas Freeman."

"And one of those five named Riley?"

"Yes, sir."

"You see him again waiting outside the church when you went for help?"

"Yes, sir," I said. "He didn't want to let me by to get Doc Harper. Said it'd serve the man right if he died."

Marshal Keaton shook his head. "Seth, the Civil War ended over nine years ago. Seems folks here want to fight it over and over again."

"Sir?"

"Freeman. You think Silas was born with that name?"

"Sir?"

"I imagine he took the name for himself the day he walked away from whoever owned him."

That thought hit me harder than any blast of snow. In Maine, slavery had only been something to listen to grown-up folks argue about.

"Seth," Marshal Keaton continued as he urged his horse into the wind, "the Sioux Indians call men like Silas buffalo soldiers. It's a term of respect for anyone as hard to bring down in a fight as a hard-charging buffalo. Silas probably fought just as hard for his freedom. You should be proud your father did what he did to help Silas."

For a couple of hundred yards, Marshal Keaton said nothing more. I waited until we'd crested a rise and were headed down to a ranch house in the shelter of some trees. "Marshal, what did you mean about my Pa's reputation?"

Silence, except for the wind.

"You're what, 16?" Marshal Keaton finally said.

"Yes, sir. Me and Pa, we ain't been seeing eye to eye lately. I got things to learn about the world, but he keeps calling me to the Bible." Which was one of the reasons I wanted the train out of Laramie so badly—to prove to the world and myself I had what it took to be on my own.

"Sixteen," Marshal Keaton said. "Old enough to have your own mind, but not old enough to see your father the way the world sees him. And just a boy during the great war. He's been quiet about his time in the Union Army?"

"Yes, sir. He hates guns. He don't like it much I want to learn to shoot."

"Folks here inquired about your father before sending him the call to preach. We heard plenty about his part in the war, all of it good. Someday, when the time's right for him, I reckon he'll tell you more. Then you might understand."

It seemed like all the answer I would get, so I nodded, knowing I'd ponder it deeply over the next while.

We were almost at the ranch house. I had one other question. "Why'd you say folks are fighting the Civil War all over again?"

Marshal Keaton dismounted from the horse and helped me down. He put his hand on my shoulder and looked me directly in the face. "Seth, if Silas Freeman were hanged by a lynch mob, he wouldn't be alive to defend himself against an accusation too many folks would believe too easily, just because his skin's a different color. And I got a feeling that would suit the Riley boys just fine."

▼ ▼ ▼ ▼ ▼

We faced Wilcombe Riley across his kitchen table. Gray-haired, he seemed mountain-big in his red flannel shirt. He had opened the door to us with a scowl and had not offered any coffee.

"With all due respect, Mr. Riley," Marshal Keaton was saying, "it's common knowledge you and your boys don't get along with Mayor Crawford."

Wilcombe Riley scowled. "Don't mean they'd shoot a man."

"I heard Crawford and his First National was going to call in your bank loan. Helps you out plenty if the man is dead."

Wilcombe Riley worked a tobacco plug at the side of his mouth. He spit a stream of juice onto the rough wood floor. "Lord works in mysterious ways, Marshal."

"Shooting and murder is the devil's work, Mr. Riley. Make no mistake about it. Where's your third boy? Adam's his name, if I recall."

"Adam's been here all afternoon, Marshal."

"I surely hope that's true, Mr. Riley. I can see it happening like this. Your three boys see Crawford in town, maybe decide in this snowstorm they can shoot him in the alley and move out quick. Only, Silas Freeman is nearby and shouts for help as they're running away. Frank gets it into his head Silas can easy carry the blame, 'specially if he's dead right on top of the mayor. Frank shoots, and Silas runs. Frank gathers up some men to lynch Silas. Jethro gets Doc Harper and Jake and me but don't tell us that Frank is chasing Silas, giving Frank time to lynch Silas, the only witness. Adam comes back here and pretends nothing happened."

"Can Crawford back up the testimony of this Silas Free-man?"

"Crawford was shot in the back. He didn't see anything," Marshal Keaton said.

Another stream of juice from the old man. "Then all you got is fancy speculation, Marshal. I'll swear in court Adam was in the house when I returned from checking cattle. That was at least an hour back, long before your mayor was shot."

I glanced at the coats on a coatrack near the door, remembering the snow that had melted on the one man's hat brim in the church. If Wilcombe Riley was telling the truth and he'd been outside, the leather of his coat would be darkened by the melted snow. Which it was, hanging on top of another coat below.

"Now, Marshal," Wilcombe said, "if you don't mind, me and Adam got some chores left in the barn."

Wilcombe Riley pushed himself back from the table, rose to his feet, and hollered for Adam, a tall, skinny man who came into the kitchen with his chin defiant and the smirk on his face clear evidence he'd been listening to this entire conversation.

Marshal Keaton looked from one to the other. He must have decided what I'd guessed. There was nothing to do here if Wilcombe Riley was prepared to swear an alibi for his son.

Marshal Keaton gave me the nod. I followed him outside.

Instead of helping me on the horse, however, he pushed me behind him and faced the door. It opened, and Wilcombe and Adam stepped into the snow.

Marshal Keaton lifted his rifle from the saddle case and walked back toward them.

"Gentlemen," he said as he levered a shell into place, "step back inside. And I ain't asking. I'm telling."

I followed the three of them back into the kitchen. Wilcombe and Adam Riley glared at the marshal, but his rifle held them silent.

"Seth," Marshal Keaton said. "Close your eyes. I've got a question. And think real careful before you answer. I need you as a witness to all this. My word alone won't be enough."

"Yes, sir. I'll do my best."

"I saw you looking over at the coats before," Marshal Keaton said. "Describe them to me."

I did.

"Open your eyes," Marshal Keaton said. "Which coat is Adam wearing?"

I saw and understood. Adam Riley wore the coat dark with melted snow, the coat that had been atop the other on the coatrack. Which meant Adam had come in *after* Wilcombe, otherwise Wilcombe's coat would have been on top, thrown on last. We'd caught Wilcombe in a lie, and there could have been only one reason for him to lie.

▼ ▼ ▼ ▼ ▼

Mayor Crawford lived.

So did Silas Freeman. His testimony alone might not have been enough to convict the Riley brothers, for Marshal Keaton had been right. Folks still were fighting the Civil War, nearly a decade after it had ended, and did not want to believe a buffalo soldier.

But I got called to witness, and between Marshal Keaton and me, we managed to show the jury how important it was that Wilcombe Riley had lied about checking the stock.

Because of it, Silas was found innocent, the Rileys guilty. By then it was summer.

As time passed, I made it a habit to stop by Marshal Keaton's office, where a pot of coffee was always waiting and where he and Jake made it clear in plenty of conversations that it isn't a gun and badge that make someone a hero. As for Pa, I got tired of waiting for him to tell me about his time in the Union Army, so I asked him flat out and found out he was a decorated war hero. Marshal Keaton was right. It gave me a new understanding of my pa, and it became easier for him and me to see eye to eye. All told, I managed to figure out heroes don't always tote pistols. And you don't have to take a train out of town to become one.

WHAT'S UP THIS WEEK?

- A Courageous Savior
- True Strength
- What's Right vs. What's Popular

PRAYER POWER

We all need courage to succeed in life. What's it made of? As we move into this week, ask God to show you his definition of courage.

A COURAGEOUS SAVIOR

Let's look at the ideal example we have of courage: Jesus.

BRAIN STRETCHERS

FOR KIDS:

1. Why was Seth surprised to watch his father show such bravery in protecting Silas Freeman? What was his opinion of his father's profession as a preacher? Did he think it was a courageous career?
2. Do you know of anyone you'd describe as courageous? Maybe there's a character on TV who fits the bill. Why do you think of that person as courageous?

ASK AN ADULT:

1. How would you define courage?
2. In what ways do you think Jesus was courageous?
3. Do you ever find it difficult to show courage?

SCRIPTURE POWER

God's weakness is far stronger than the greatest of human strength.
(1 Corinthians 1:25)

True courage comes from God, and he's where we need to begin our discussion. No one is more powerful than God. He created and maintains the whole universe. He doesn't shrink back from opposition, and he always wins. Not only that, but he knows how to show gentle strength. God could squash anyone like a bug. But instead, he sent his son, Jesus, as a baby to save the world. God's a God with guts!

> We are joined together in [Christ's] body by his strong sinews, and we grow only as we get our nourishment and strength from God. (Colossians 2:19)

Those of us who have accepted Christ as our Savior are part of God's family. One of the benefits we have because of this is God's strength at our disposal. This verse describes Christ as having strong sinews, which are like ligaments. We have a powerful, courageous Savior as the source of our strength. Knowing that should give us all the courage we need to face life's challenges.

> May the Lord make your love grow and overflow to each other and to everyone else, just as our love overflows toward you. As a result, Christ will make your hearts strong, blameless, and holy when you stand before God our Father on that day when our Lord Jesus comes with all those who belong to him. (1 Thessalonians 3:12-13)

Because of the love we know in Christ, we can have the strength and blamelessness to stand before God. Our secure place in him is unshakable. We can move forward in our daily life with courage.

PRAYER POWER

Thank God today for giving you such a great example of courage in Jesus. Think about the ways Jesus showed courage in his life. Commit to following his pattern of gentle strength and being willing to be unpopular if necessary because you stand up for what's right.

TRUE STRENGTH

Jesus showed true strength often by his gentleness toward children and those who couldn't defend themselves. Silas Freeman may have been physically powerful and courageous, but society kept him from being able to defend himself. Seth's father showed courage and true strength by standing up for Silas and giving him a fair deal. Let's talk more about true strength.

BRAIN STRETCHERS

FOR KIDS:

1. How do you think Seth defined true strength? Do you think his normally quiet father was strong?
2. Do you think the Riley brothers thought they had true strength? Did their wickedness make them strong or weak?

ASK AN ADULT:

1. Which do you think is more important: physical strength or a strong character?
2. Does a person need to be physically strong to be courageous? Why or why not?

SCRIPTURE POWER

It is not by force nor by strength, but by my Spirit, says the Lord Almighty. (Zechariah 4:6)

Yesterday we talked about Jesus as the perfect example of courage. This verse goes right along with that, because it shows that true strength comes from God. Seth's father didn't use force, like the Rileys did, to make his point. An injustice was being done in God's house when the Rileys stormed in, and Seth's father knew he had a responsibility to stand up for Silas and give him a chance to explain what happened. The Rileys' prejudiced hatred for Silas was wrong, but God gave Seth's father the courage he needed to react with truly courageous strength.

I pray that from his glorious, unlimited resources he will give you mighty inner strength through his Holy Spirit. (Ephesians 3:16)

God is the source of courage and strength, and his resources are freely at our disposal when we need them. Think about it: we have the strength of almighty God fighting for us. There's no reason for us to question our courage.

The righteous will move onward and forward, and those with pure hearts will become stronger and stronger. (Job 17:9)

God considers his children righteous, and God supplies his children with his strength. Therefore, we can move forward courageously in life, without shrinking back. As we know God better and grow in his righteousness, we will become more aware of how his power works in us.

PRAYER POWER

Spend time alone with God, and ask him to show you more about what true strength is. He'll reveal it to you when you ask. When we're faithful to spend time with God, his character will become ours, and we'll reflect his true strength.

WHAT'S RIGHT VS. WHAT'S POPULAR

Courage is essential when it comes to standing up for what's right, even when the right view is not the popular one.

BRAIN STRETCHERS

FOR KIDS:

1. Many people wouldn't have stood up for Silas because of his skin color. What does God think of that view? Do you know anyone who is prejudiced? What do you think of that person's opinion?
2. What are some right values that many people you know don't agree with?

ASK AN ADULT:

1. Why do other people sometimes make it difficult for us to do what's right?
2. Have you ever been in a situation where you knew what was right, even though it seemed everyone else disagreed with you? What did you do? What happened?

SCRIPTURE POWER

Be on guard. Stand true to what you believe. Be coura-geous. Be strong. (1 Corinthians 16:13)

This verse calls us to be true to what we believe. Doing that takes courage, but we have a great example to follow of characters in the Bible who showed courage despite horrible treatment from others. God doesn't call us to fit in with the crowd. He calls us to be true to him.

May our Lord Jesus Christ and God our Father, who loved us and in his special favor gave us everlasting comfort and good hope, comfort your hearts and give you strength in every good thing you do and say. (2 Thessa-lonians 2:16-17)

God's comfort and strength will come "in every good thing [we] do and say." That means that we must choose to do what's right, and as we follow through, God will provide his strength. We must take the risk of being courageous; then God will bless our efforts.

Stand your ground, putting on the sturdy belt of truth and the body armor of God's righteousness. (Ephesians 6:14)

The Bible is full of encouragement and commands to give us strength and courage. When we're living in Christ, God's righteousness is like strong armor. His truth helps us stand our ground when the pressure threatens to weaken us. Stand strong! That's God's battle cry to us.

We have faithfully preached the truth. God's power has been working in us. We have righteousness as our

weapon, both to attack and to defend ourselves.
(2 Corinthians 6:7)

Here's another verse that shows God's righteousness as a weapon. It can take the offensive position to attack wrongdoing, or it can be used defensively, to protect what we know to be right and true. When we rely on God for courage and true strength, and when we know we're walking in his truth, our courage can be limitless.

PRAYER POWER

No matter what situations you may be facing now that demand your courage, know that God is ready to fight with you. Tell him what's on your mind, and ask him to give you strength to fight for what's right, even when it's unpopular.

CONCLUDING THOUGHTS

Seth learned a lot about courage by watching his father handle the Silas Freeman incident. He thought a true hero was someone who was tough— like the "pistol-toting marshal" he was determined to become.

Seth learned that courage is often found in quiet strength. His preacher father always had courage; he just chose wisely to have a strong character in Christ ahead of being a musclebound thug like each of the Rileys. When push came to shove, Seth's dad had all the courage he needed because he knew God's truth was behind him. He had righteousness on his side, and he was determined to fight for someone who wasn't in a position to defend himself.

Sometimes our courage can waver because we forget the power we have as Christians. God has given his promises for strength to his children. When he calls us to something, he promises to give us everything we need to carry out his will.

Life in Christ is a courageous journey. Is your courage ready for the adventure?

LINE IT UP!

Talk some more with your family or Bible study friends about
some of the problems with society's values that don't line up
with God's truth. Discuss how God's truth is so much better
than the world's view of things. What would life be like if we
didn't have the Bible as a foundation of right and wrong? Ask
each other why you think people don't like to hear about
what's right and wrong. How can we hurt each other when
we ignore God's commands? Fellowshipping with one
another gives us courage and encouragement to help us
know we're not alone.

PRAYER POWER

How's your courage in standing up for what's right? Does it
need improvement? Do you want to be a person of courage?
Ask God to help you work on that characteristic, and trust
that his strength will be there for you as you stand up for
what's right. God bless!